CAMBRIDGE SCHOOL

*Chaucer*

# THE
# *Nun's Priest's*
# PROLOGUE AND TALE

Edited by Elizabeth Huddlestone

**CAMBRIDGE**
UNIVERSITY PRESS

The publishers would like to thank Professor Helen Cooper for her help in the preparation of this edition.

CAMBRIDGE UNIVERSITY PRESS
Cambridge, New York, Melbourne, Madrid, Cape Town, Singapore, São Paulo, Delhi

Cambridge University Press
The Edinburgh Building, Cambridge CB2 8RU, UK

www.cambridge.org
Information on this title: www.cambridge.org/9780521786546

First published 2000
4th printing 2008

Printed in the United Kingdom at the University Press, Cambridge

*A catalogue record for this publication is available from the British Library*

ISBN 978-0-521-78654-6 paperback

Prepared for publication by Elizabeth Paren
Designed and formatted by Geoffrey Wadsley
Illustrated by William Geldart
Picture research by Valerie Mulcahy

*Thanks are due to the following for permission to reproduce photographs:*
The Bodleian Library, University of Oxford, pages 24 (MS Ashmole 1462), 56 (MS Douce 332,
fol.58r); The Bridgeman Art Library/Private Collection, page 14; Cambridge University Library,
page 76; English Heritage Photo Library, page 75; The Fotomas Index, page 72; Glasgow University
Library, page 26 (MS Hunter 252, fol.70r); Hulton Getty Picture Collection, pages 7, 40, 68;
Tom Mackie, page 17; Magnum Photos/Jean Gaumy, page 66; Theartarchive/British Library,
page 65; Topham Picturepoint, pages 34, 38, 44.
For cover photograph: Canterbury Tales: The Nun's Priest's Tale, *Ellesmere Manuscript* (Facsimile
Edition 1911), Theartarchive/V & A Museum, London.
The extract on page 76 is reprinted from Geoffrey of Vinsauf, *Poetria Nova*, trans. Margaret F. Nims,
by permission of the publisher © 1967 by the Pontifical Institute of Medieval Studies, Toronto.

# Contents

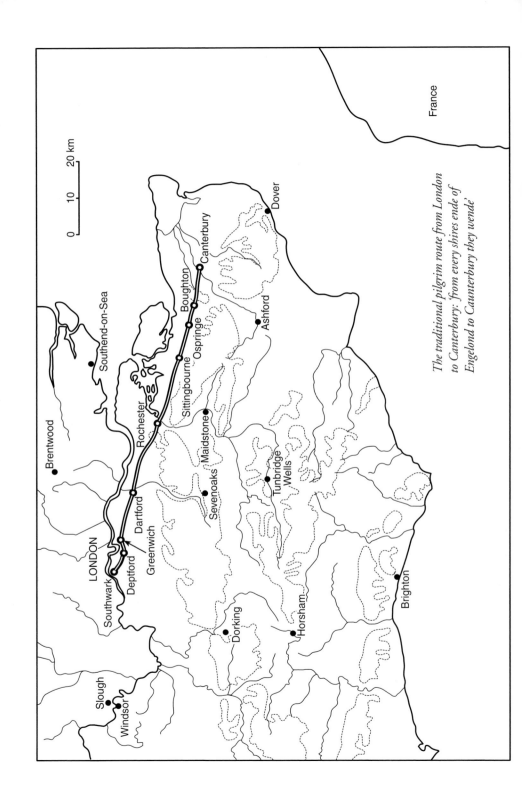

The traditional pilgrim route from London to Canterbury: 'from every shires ende of Engelond to Caunterbury they wende'

# Introduction

The first encounter with a page of Chaucer in its original form can be a disconcerting experience. Initially, few words look familiar. Even when the meaning has been puzzled out, the reader is faced with an account of people who lived and died in a world very different from our own. The fourteenth century seems very far away, and you might be forgiven for thinking that *The Canterbury Tales* are 'too difficult'.

The aim of this series is, therefore, to introduce you to the world of Chaucer in a way that will make medieval language and life as accessible as possible. With this in mind, we have adopted a layout in which each right-hand page of text is headed by a brief summary of content, and faced by a left-hand page offering a glossary of more difficult words and phrases, as well as commentary notes dealing with style, characterisation and other relevant information. There are illustrations, and suggestions for ways in which you might become involved in the text to help make it come alive.

If initial hurdles are lowered in this way, Chaucer's wit and irony, his ability to suggest character and caricature, and his delight in raising provocative and challenging issues from various standpoints, can more readily be appreciated and enjoyed. There is something peculiarly delightful in discovering that someone who lived six hundred years ago had a sense of humour and a grasp of personalities and relationships as fresh and relevant today as it was then.

Each tale provides considerable material for fruitful discussion of fourteenth century attitudes and modern parallels. It is important to realise that the views expressed by the teller of any one tale are not necessarily Chaucer's own. Many of the activities suggested are intended to make you aware of the multiplicity of voices and attitudes in *The Canterbury Tales*. A considerable part of the enjoyment comes from awareness of the tongue-in-cheek presence of the author, who allows his characters to speak for themselves, thereby revealing their weaknesses and obsessions.

Essential information contained in each book includes a brief explanation of what *The Canterbury Tales* are, followed by some hints on handling the language. There is then a brief introduction to the teller of the relevant story, his or her portrait from the General Prologue, and an initial investigation into the techniques Chaucer uses to present characters.

The left-hand page commentaries give information applicable to the text. Finally, each book offers a full list of pilgrims, further information on Chaucer's own life and works, some background history, and greater discussion of specific medieval issues. Suggestions for essays and themes to be explored are also included. On page 80 there is a relatively short glossary of words most frequently encountered in the text, to supplement the more detailed glossary on each page.

Chaucer's tales are witty, clever and approachable, and raise interesting parallels with life today. His manipulation of the short story form is masterly. We hope this edition will bring *The Canterbury Tales* alive and allow you to appreciate Chaucer's art with ease and enjoyment.

# What are The Canterbury Tales?

They are a collection of stories, loosely linked together, apparently told by a variety of storytellers with very different characters and from different social classes. In fact, both the storytellers themselves and the tales are the creation of one man, Geoffrey Chaucer. Chaucer imagines a group of pilgrims, setting off from the Tabard Inn one spring day on the long journey from London to the shrine of St Thomas Becket in Canterbury – a journey that on horseback would take about four days.

To make time pass more pleasantly they agree to tell stories to one another. Chaucer begins by introducing his pilgrims to the reader, in descriptions which do much to reveal the characters, vices and virtues of each individual. We learn more from the way each person introduces his or her tale, still more from the tales themselves and the way in which each one is told, and even further information is offered by the manner in which some pilgrims react to what others have to say. By this means Chaucer provides a witty, penetrating insight into the attitudes, weaknesses, virtues and preoccupations of English men and women of the fourteenth century. Some of their behaviour and interests may seem very strange to modern readers; at other times they seem just like us.

## THE TALES

Although Chaucer never completed *The Canterbury Tales*, enough of it was completed for us to appreciate the richness of texture and ironical comment Chaucer wove into his tapestry of fourteenth century life. The tales themselves are quite simple – medieval audiences did not expect original plots, but rather clever or unexpected ways of telling stories that might already be known in another form. Chaucer's audiences of educated friends, witty and urbane courtiers, perhaps the highest aristocracy, and even the king and queen, were clearly able to appreciate his skills to the full. Story telling was a leisurely process, since reading was a social rather than a private activity. Since many people could not read, Chaucer would expect the tales to be read aloud. You could try to read them like this – you will find advice on pronunciation on page 9 – and you will discover they become still more lively and dramatic when spoken rather than just read on the page.

Most of the tales in the collection include aspects of at least one of the following categories of tales familiar to Chaucer's audience.

**Courtly romances** These stories of courtly love affairs were for the upper classes. They often told of unrequited love from a distance, the male lover suffering sleepless nights of anguish, pining away, writing poetry, serenading his beloved with love songs and performing brave feats of noble daring. Meanwhile the beloved (but untouchable) lady would sit in her bower and sew, walk in her castle gardens, set her lover impossible tasks to accomplish, and give him a scarf or a handkerchief as a keepsake.

**Fabliaux** Extended jokes or tricks, often bawdy, and usually full of sexual innuendo.

*The destination of the pilgrims – Canterbury Cathedral today*

**Fables** These are tales that make a moral point, often using animals as characters.

**Sermons** Sermons were stories with a moral message. Since 95 per cent of society could not read, sermons had to be good, interesting and full of dramatic story-telling. The line between a good story and a good sermon was very thin indeed. Usually there was an abstract theme (gluttony, avarice, pride) and much use was made of biblical and classical parallels or *exempla* to underline the preacher's point.

**Confessions** The story-tellers often look back over their own lives, revealing faults and unhappinesses to the audience. This aspect is usually introduced in the teller's prologue to the actual story.

The tales vary widely in content and tone, since medieval stories, Chaucer's included, were supposed both to instruct and to entertain. Many have an underlying moral; some, such as the Pardoner's Tale, are highly dramatic, and others, like those told by the Knight and the Squire, have their origins firmly in the courtly love tradition. Many are more complex than this suggests. They also vary greatly: Chaucer includes stories as sentimental as that of the Prioress, and as crude and bawdy as those of the Miller and the Reeve.

The device of using different characters to tell different tales allows Chaucer to distance himself from what is being said, and to disguise the fact that he controls the varied and opinionated voices of his creations. He can pretend, for instance, to have no way of preventing the drunken Miller from telling his vulgar story about the carpenter's wife, and he can absolve himself from blame when the tellers become sexually explicit. A modern audience may find his frankness and openness about sex surprising, but it was understandable, for there was little privacy, even for the well-to-do, and sexual matters were no secret. The coarse satire of the fabliaux was as much enjoyed by Chaucer's 'gentil' audience as the more restrained romances.

# Chaucer's language

The unfamiliar appearance of a page of Chaucerian English often prevents students from pursuing their investigations any further. It does no good telling them that this man used language with a complexity and subtlety not found in any writer of English anywhere before him. They remain unimpressed. He looks incomprehensible.

In fact, with a little help, it does not take very long to master Chaucer's language. Much of the vocabulary is the same, or at least very similar to, words we use today. On page 80 there is a glossary of the unfamiliar words most frequently used in this text, and these will quickly become familiar. Other words and phrases that could cause difficulties are explained on the page facing the actual text.

The language of Chaucer is known as Middle English – a term covering English as it was written and spoken in the period roughly between 1150 and 1500. It is difficult to be more precise than this, for Middle English itself was changing and developing throughout that period towards 'modern' English.

Old English (Anglo-Saxon) was spoken and written until around 1066, the time of the Norman Conquest. This event put power in England into the hands of the Norman lords, who spoke their own brand of Norman French. Inevitably this became the language of the upper classes. The effect was felt in the church, for speedily the control of the monasteries and nunneries was given to members of the new French-speaking aristocracy. Since these religious houses were the seats of learning and centres of literacy, the effect on language was considerable. If you were a wealthy Anglo-Saxon, eager to get on in the world of your new over-lords, you learnt French. Many people were bi- or even trilingual: French was the language of the law courts and much international commerce; Latin was the language of learning (from elementary learning to the highest levels of scholarship) and the church (from parish church services to the great international institution of the papacy).

Gradually, as inter-marriage between Norman French and English families became more common, the distinction between the two groups and the two languages became blurred. Many French words became absorbed into Old English, making it more like the language we speak today. In the thirteenth century King John lost control of his Norman lands, and as hostility between England and France grew, a sense of English nationalism strengthened. In 1362 the English language was used for the first time in an English parliament. At the same time, Geoffrey Chaucer, a young ex-prisoner of war, was sharpening his pens and his wit, testing the potential for amusement, satire and beauty in this rich, infinitely variable, complex literary tool.

Although some tales are partly, or entirely, in prose, *The Canterbury Tales* are written largely in rhyming iambic couplets. This form of regular metre and rhyme is flexible enough to allow Chaucer to write in a range of styles. He uses the couplet form to imitate colloquial speech as easily as philosophical debate. Most importantly, Chaucer wrote poetry 'for the ear'; it is written for the listener, as much as for the reader. Rhyme and alliteration add emphasis and link ideas and objects together in a way that is satisfying for the audience. The words jog along as easily and comfortably as the imaginary pilgrims and their horses jogged to Canterbury.

## PRONUNCIATION

Chaucer spoke the language of London, of the king's court, but he was well aware of differences in dialect and vocabulary in other parts of the country. In the Reeve's Tale, for instance, he mocks the north country accents of the two students. It is clear, therefore, that there were differences in pronunciation in the fourteenth century, just as there are today.

Having been told that Chaucer wrote verse to be read aloud, students may be dismayed to find that they do not know how it should sound. There are two encouraging things to bear in mind. The first is that although scholars feel fairly sure they know something about how Middle English sounded, they cannot be certain, and a number of different readings can still be heard. The second concerns the strong metrical and rhyming structure Chaucer employed in the writing of his Tales.

**Finding the rhythm**  Follow the rhythm of the verse (iambic pentameter), sounding or omitting the final 'e' syllable in the word as seems most appropriate. In the line

    **Whan that the brighte sonne gan to springe,**

it would add an unnecessary syllable if the final 'e' in 'springe' were to be pronounced. An 'e' at the end of a word almost always disappears if it is followed by a word beginning with 'h' or a vowel.

In the case of these examples:

    **I sette nat a straw by thy dremynges,**

and

    **And thus he seyde unto us everichon,**

the best swing to the regular 10-syllabled line is achieved by sounding the 'e' (as a neutral vowel sound, like the 'u' in 'put', or the 'a' in 'about') in the word 'sette', but not in 'seyde'.

**Other points**  In words beginning with the letter 'y' (for example 'ywet', 'yknowe') the 'y' is sounded as it would be in the modern 'party'. Many consonants now silent were pronounced – as in 'knight', 'wrong'. All the consonants would be given voice in words such as 'brighte' and 'fighte', and the 'gh' would be sounded like the Scots 'ch' in 'loch'. The combination 'ow' (for example 'yow', meaning 'you') is pronounced as 'how', and the 'ei' in 'streit' would be like the 'a' sound in 'pay'.

For more ideas of what the language might have sounded like, listen to the tapes of Chaucer published by Cambridge University Press and by the 'Chaucer Man' (Trevor Eaton).

## WARM-UP ACTIVITIES

• Choose a long, self-contained section from the text. Lines 14-39 of The Nun's Priest's Prologue and lines 609-35 (the chase) are useful examples. After a brief explanation of the content, if necessary, students work in pairs, speaking alternately, and changing over at each punctuation point. It should be possible to develop a fair turn of speed without losing the sense of the passage.

- Alternatively, the whole group walks around the room, speaking the text and changing direction at each punctuation mark.
- Again in pairs: while one person beats out a steady rhythm on a table [^/^/^/^/^/^/] the partner reads out the text to fit the rhythm.

## GRAMMATICAL POINTS

**Emphatic negatives**  Usually, someone stating, 'I'm not having nothing to do with it' would be saying the opposite of what was intended: the two negatives cancel each other out. Chaucer uses double or triple negatives quite often to build up the strength of his argument. For example, in The Nun's Priest's Tale the fox is trying to flatter Chauntecleer by praising the cockerel's father:

> **That ther nas no man in no regioun**
> **That him in song or wisdom mighte passe.**

The repeated negative strengthens the force of what is being said. In some modern English dialects double negatives are still used, for example that of London Cockney speakers.

**Word elision**  In modern written English words and phrases are often run together (elided) to represent the spoken form of these words: 'didn't', 'can't', 'won't', 'I've', and so on. Chaucer uses short forms of words too, especially in forming the negative. In his time it was usual to form a negative by placing 'ne' before the verb. With common verbs this was often elided into the verb. Thus 'ne was' is the Chaucerian form of 'was not', but it was often written as 'nas'. Similarly, 'noot' means 'do not know'.

**The 'y' prefix**  The past participle of a verb sometimes has a 'y' before the rest of the verb, particularly when the verb is passive.

| | |
|---|---|
| **he hath a corn yfounde** | he found a grain of corn |
| **ywarned by thy dremes** | warned by your dreams |

**The 'possessive' form of nouns**  In modern English, we use an apostrophe to show possession: 'a son of the priest' becomes 'a priest's son'. Middle English had a particular formation that is still used in modern German. Where we now use an apostrophe followed by an 's', Chaucer used the suffix 'es', so 'a priest's son' is 'a preestes sone', the '-es' becoming an extra syllable.

**Construction of sentences**  The word order in Chaucer is often different from modern English, which can make it a little more difficult to understand, but it is easy to get used to. In this sentence, for example, the verb is at the end:

> **I can noon harm of no womman divine.**
> I can imagine no harm from any woman.

In this example, the two halves of the sentence would be reversed in modern English:

> **Of poynaunt sauce hir neded never a deel.**
> She had no need of any strongly flavoured sauce.

# The Nun's Priest's contribution

Chaucer promises at the beginning of *The Canterbury Tales* that he will describe all his pilgrims, telling the audience something of their status and their personality. He lists them in rough order of precedence, beginning with the Knight and his party (his son, the Squire, and their Yeoman servant). He continues with the group of religious characters who have status and importance (the Prioress, the Monk and the Friar), and then moves down through the social ranks, listing well-to-do middle class individuals and those with some wealth, followed by more lowly commoners. He ends his list with two unashamedly corrupt servants of the church, the Summoner and the Pardoner. This introduction is named in some early manuscripts of *The Canterbury Tales* as 'The General Prologue'. A list of the pilgrims who feature in the complete work may be found on pages 65-6.

The Nun's Priest appears at the end of the description of the Prioress, who features immediately after the Knight's group. The description of the Prioress can be found on page 62. The General Prologue says the Prioress has with her another nun, serving as her secretary/personal assistant, and 'preestes thre'. This seems unlikely. One priest would have been quite sufficient and it is possible that the second part of this line was written by someone other than Chaucer, and that 'thre' simply made an appropriate rhyme. It is likely that the convent group was completed by two more nuns. At the convent the Nun's Priest would be responsible for giving Holy Communion and other sacraments, and preaching – not duties which women were allowed to perform.

There is no description of the Nun's Priest in The General Prologue so the reader must pick up clues to his character from his tale, and its prologue and epilogue. In spite of his anonymity in The General Prologue, his contribution is one of the most beautifully crafted tales in the collection. It certainly shows a man of learning.

Chaucer never completed *The Canterbury Tales* but he left the tales he had finished clustered into groups. The Nun's Priest's Tale comes into a 'fragment' which includes tales from the Shipman, Chaucer, the Prioress and the Monk. One scholar has given these tales the title of 'the Literature Group', since they each in some way explore the double functions of literature: to teach and to entertain, 'doctrine' and 'desport'.

The Nun's Priest's Tale fulfils both functions well, as you will find. The Host tells him his story has to be 'myrie', but he manages to include much 'sentence' (meaning). For example, there are long and deep debates on the important topics of predestination and the significance of dreams, but since they are being discussed by chickens we are invited to laugh at the whole concept of debate.

When you have studied the whole Tale you may want to decide what its 'moralitee' (moral) is, but it is so cleverly crafted that there are several different conclusions which could be drawn.

- The Host, Harry Bailey of the Tabard Inn, is in charge of the tale telling, but the Monk's efforts at entertaining the pilgrims are so miserable that the Knight cannot stop himself intervening. In his cell the Monk has copies of a hundred tragedies and before the Knight stops him is coming to the end of the seventeenth (about King Croesus), having begun with the fall of Lucifer. What does his intervention suggest about the Knight's personality and how he sees his role amongst the other pilgrims?
- Look at the change in language and tone when the Host begins to speak. Why do you think Chaucer has done this?

The Knight, the Monk and the Host all use 'ye/yow' (you) when addressing each other. The Nun's Priest is addressed as 'thou', indicating his lower social status.

In lines 15-16 the Host is quoting from the Monk's final story,

> **Tragedies noon oother maner thyng**
> **Ne kan in syngyn crie ne biwaille**
> **But that Fortune alwey wole assaille**
> **With unwar strook the regnes that been proude;**
> **For whan men trusteth hire, thanne wol she faille,**
> **And covere hir brighte face with a clowde.**

The Host pretends not to understand the final line, which could be interpreted as 'Fortune changes suddenly, in the same way that the sun goes behind a cloud'. Medieval people often pictured the unpredictable changes of Fortune as a blind-folded woman spinning a wheel onto which everyone clung. Much time was spent debating how the arbitrary nature of Fortune fitted in with God's benevolent plan for the universe. The role of Fortune is important in the Tale. For example, see lines 233-4 and 637-38. (For a picture of blind-folded Fortune see page 56.)

| | | | |
|---|---|---|---|
| 1 | **Hoo** stop [The Knight, as the most senior person present, interrupts the Monk politely, but pointedly. The Host is the master of ceremonies, but does not step forward at this moment.] | 14 | **Seint Poules** St Paul's Cathedral, London |
| | | 15 | **clappeth** chatters [This picks up the reference to the bell of St Paul's.] |
| 3-4 | **for litel hevinesse/Is right ynough to muche folk, I gesse** a small amount of grief is enough for most people I imagine | 18 | **pardee** certainly |
| | | 19 | **biwaille** complain, lament |
| | | 20 | **als** also |
| | | 22 | **so God yow blesse** as God may bless you |
| 5 | **disese** displeasure | 23 | **anoyeth** displeases |
| 8 | **solas** solace, delight | 24 | **Swich talking is nat worth a boter-flye** what you say is worth less than a butterfly |
| 10 | **wexeth** becomes, grows | | |
| 12 | **Swich thing is gladsom, as it thinketh me** such a thing is pleasing, it seems to me [Note the use of the impersonal verb here.] | 25 | **desport ne game** entertainment or pleasure |

*The Knight interrupts the Monk, saying that he dislikes stories of bad fortune and prefers to hear of people who are successful. The Host joins in, dismissing the Monk's Tale as mere 'hevinesse', and requesting something better from the Nun's Priest.*

'Hoo,' quod the Knight, 'good sire, namoore of this!
That ye han seyd is right ynough, ywis,
And muchel moore; for litel hevinesse
Is right ynough to muche folk, I gesse.
I seye for me, it is a greet disese,                                    5
Whereas men han been in greet welthe and ese,
To heeren of hire sodeyn fal, allas,
And the contrarie is joye and greet solas,
As whan a man hath been in povre estaat,
And climbeth up and wexeth fortunat,                                   10
And there abideth in prosperitee.
Swich thing is gladsom, as it thinketh me,
And of swich thing were goodly for to telle.'
'Ye,' quod oure Hooste, 'by Seint Poules belle,
Ye seye right sooth; this Monk he clappeth lowde.                      15
He spak how "Fortune covered with a clowde"
I noot nevere what; and als of a "tragedie"
Right now ye herde, and, pardee, no remedie
It is for to biwaille ne compleyne
That that is doon, and als it is a peyne,                              20
As ye han seyd, to heere of hevinesse.
    Sire Monk, namoore of this, so God yow blesse,
Youre tale anoyeth al this compaignye.
Swich talking is nat worth a boterflye,
For therinne is ther no desport ne game.                              25

In The General Prologue (lines 165-207) we learn that the Monk is an 'outrider' who visits the outlying cells of his monastery. He obviously relishes life outside the mother-house, where rules are not observed so strictly, and he enjoys riding and hunting. His food and his appearance are important to him and there is even a hint that he enjoys other earthly pleasures, for to fasten his hood he has a gold pin with a 'love-knotte'. The Host attacks the Monk very strongly, showing his disappointment at the contrast between the cheerful teller and his depressing tale.

- Re-read lines 22-4. Who is speaking here? What light do you think these three lines throw on lines 44-51?
- As you read through The Nun's Priest's Tale, make notes so that you can decide how far the Priest has satisfied the demands of the Knight and of the Host in his story.

| | |
|---|---|
| 26 | **Daun Piers** Sir Peter [In the Monk's Prologue the Host says he does not know the Monk's name, and suggests calling him John, Thomas or Alban.] |
| 27 | **hertely** sincerely |
| 28 | **sikerly** surely |
| | **nere** were it not for [ne were] |
| 30-2 | **By hevene king ... so deep** by the King of Heaven [Jesus Christ] who died for all of us, I should have fallen down asleep however deep the muddy holes in the road were |
| 34 | **clerkes** scholars |
| 35-6 | **Whereas ... his sentence** if a man has no-one listening to him, there is no point in speaking on his subject matter |

| | |
|---|---|
| 37-8 | **And wel ... reported be** I can take in the essence of what I hear, if it is well told [This is rather ironic, since the Host often misunderstands what he hears.] |
| 40 | **no lust to pleye** no inclination to amuse |
| 43 | **anon** immediately |
| 44 | **neer** closer |
| 46 | **blithe** happy |
| | **jade** nag, worn-out horse |
| 48 | **rekke nat a bene** don't care a bean [a more commonplace comparison than line 24] |
| 50-1 | **'Yis, sir,' ... be blamed'** 'Yes sir', he said. 'Yes Host. As I hope to live – unless I am merry, I will certainly be blamed.' [The Nun's Priest seems intimidated by what he has just heard.] |
| 52 | **attamed** begun |
| 54 | **Sir John** [John was a common name for a priest and may not be this man's real name. 'Sir' was often used as a title for a priest. It does not mean that he has been knighted.] |

*The Nun's Priest as depicted in the Ellesmere manuscript. This was written and decorated in the fifteenth century but reproduced the style of dress of the 1380s*

*The Host says that the Monk's tale has been so boring that he was kept awake only by the noise of all the bells hanging from a bridle on the Monk's horse (as mentioned in The General Prologue). He suggests a tale about hunting but the Monk refuses, so he asks the Nun's Priest for a cheerful story. The Priest agrees.*

Wherfore, sire Monk, or Daun Piers by youre name,
I pray yow hertely telle us somwhat elles;
For sikerly, nere clinking of youre belles,
That on your bridel hange on every side,
By hevene king, that for us alle dyde,                              30
I sholde er this han fallen doun for sleep,
Althogh the slough had never been so deep;
Thanne hadde your tale al be toold in veyn.
For certeinly, as that thise clerkes seyn,
Whereas a man may have noon audience,                              35
Noght helpeth it to tellen his sentence.
   And wel I woot the substance is in me,
If any thing shal wel reported be.
Sir, sey somwhat of hunting, I yow preye.'
'Nay,' quod this Monk, 'I have no lust to pleye.                    40
Now lat another telle, as I have toold.'
Thanne spak oure Hoost with rude speche and boold,
And seyde unto the Nonnes Preest anon,
'Com neer, thou preest, com hider, thou Sir John,
Telle us swich thing as may oure hertes glade.                      45
Be blithe, though thou ride upon a jade.
What thogh thyn hors be bothe foul and lene?
If he wol serve thee, rekke nat a bene.
Looke that thyn herte be murie everemo.'
   'Yis, sir,' quod he, 'yis, Hoost, so moot I go,                  50
But I be myrie, ywis I wol be blamed.'
And right anon his tale he hath attamed,
And thus he seyde unto us everichon,
This sweete preest, this goodly man, Sir John.

- Look at the description of the Prioress from The General Prologue (pages 62-3). Make a list of points of comparison between her and the widow to see how the Prioress is being satirised for her inability to live the simple life of a nun. What do you think is the effect of the phrase 'ful simple' in each description?
- As you study the Tale, watch out for further indications of the attitude of the Nun's Priest to the Prioress and to women in general.
- This opening passage is one of the most poetic and certainly one of the most detailed in *The Canterbury Tales*. The sometimes conversational nature of the phrasing, for example 'as it were' (line 80) suggests a calm and confident speaker. Try reading it aloud before studying the language. Words such as 'narwe', and 'slendre' show the poverty of the widow's lifestyle. Consider why the grand terms 'halle' and 'bour' are used to describe the widow's main room and bedroom in her humble cottage.

| 55 | **somdeel stape in age** somewhat advanced in age |
| 56 | **whilom** once upon a time |
| | **narwe** small [*literally:* narrow] |
| 59 | **Sin thilke ... wyf** since that day she became a widow |
| 61 | **litel ... rente** her property and income were small |
| 62 | **housbondrie** economical house-keeping |
| 63 | **foond** provided for |
| 65 | **keen** cows |
| | **highte** was called |
| 66 | **bour** bedroom |
| 68 | **poynaunt** spicy |
| | **never a deel** none at all |
| 70 | **accordant to hir cote** on the same level of simplicity as her cottage |

| 71 | **repleccioun** over-eating |
| 72 | **attempree** moderate |
| | **phisik** medicine |
| 73 | **hertes suffisaunce** a contented heart |
| 74-5 | **The goute ... hir heed** Gout never prevented her from dancing and apoplexy never harmed her head. [Medieval doctors believed that plain food, eaten in moderation, was the key to good health. The illness apoplexy is caused by blood rushing to the head – perhaps the result of a rich and excessive diet. Gout can be caused by eating too much meat.] |
| 77 | **bord** table |
| 78 | **foond** found |
| 79 | **seynd** grilled |
| | **ey** egg |
| 80 | **a maner deye** a sort of dairy maid |

*A poor widow and her two daughters live a simple life. She has a small cottage and owns a few animals. She eats a plain diet and works as a dairy maid to supplement her income.*

    A povre widwe, somdeel stape in age          55
Was whilom dwelling in a narwe cotage,
Biside a grove, stondinge in a dale.
This widwe, of which I telle yow my tale,
Sin thilke day that she was last a wyf,
In pacience ladde a ful simple lyf,          60
For litel was hir catel and hir rente.
By housbondrie of swich as God hire sente
She foond hirself and eek hir doghtren two.
Thre large sowes hadde she, and namo,
Three keen, and eek a sheep that highte Malle.     65
Ful sooty was hire bour and eek hir halle,
In which she eet ful many a sklendre meel.
Of poynaunt sauce hir neded never a deel.
No deyntee morsel passed thurgh hir throte;
Hir diete was accordant to hir cote.          70
Repleccioun ne made hire nevere sik;
Attempree diete was al hir phisik,
And exercise, and hertes suffisaunce.
The goute lette hire nothing for to daunce,
N'apoplexie shente nat hir heed.          75
No wyn ne drank she, neither whit ne reed;
Hir bord was served moost with whit and blak,—
Milk and broun breed, in which she foond no lak,
Seynd bacoun, and somtime an ey or tweye;
For she was, as it were, a maner deye.         80

*'Biside a grove, stondinge in a dale'. Ancient trees in Hatfield Forest*

The colours chosen for Chauntecleer are taken from heraldry, and some are also liturgical colours used in church services – red altar coverings, for example, are used from Palm Sunday until the day before Good Friday. Chauntecleer thus appears as a high status figure.

- The description of Chauntecleer follows the rules of rhetoric (see page 76). The characterisation of Chauntecleer and Pertelote is in accordance with ideas of nobility and chivalry. Make a note of the vocabulary used to describe both birds, to emphasise their 'gentil' status.
- What point is Chaucer making by the strong contrast between the magnificence of Chauntecleer and the poverty and modesty of his widowed owner? Use this approach – and some of the techniques of rhetoric – to write your own description of two contrasting figures whose paths cross. Perhaps a politician and Mother Teresa meet at a conference, or a member of a royal family visits a day care centre for senior citizens.

| | |
|---|---|
| 82 | **withoute** outside |
| 83 | **hight** called |
| 84 | **nas his peer** he had no equal |
| 85-6 | **His voys ... chirche gon** his voice was more tuneful than the merry pleasing organs that are played in church on feast days |
| | **messe-dayes** times when lay people were allowed to attend mass |
| | **orgon** [plural] |
| 87 | **sikerer** more reliable |
| | **logge** lodgings, his perch |
| 88 | **orlogge** clock |
| 89-90 | **By nature ... thilke town** [The medieval belief was that cocks crowed every hour. The Priest describes Chauntecleer's ability in astronomical terms. He knew exactly when the sun had moved fifteen degrees, as measured at the equinox.] |
| 92 | **amended** bettered, made more accurate |
| 94 | **batailled** notched like battlements |
| 95 | **byle** bill, beak |
| | **jeet** jet |

| | |
|---|---|
| 96 | **asure** azure, sky blue |
| | **toon** toes |
| 98 | **burned** burnished, polished |
| 99 | **gentil** noble [Gentillesse is a very important concept in medieval culture and is difficult to define briefly. It includes the idea of high worth in birth as well as a character of morality and sensitivity.] |
| | **governaunce** control |
| 100 | **plesaunce** pleasure |
| 101 | **sustres and his paramours** sisters and mistresses/lovers |
| 103 | **hewed** coloured |
| 104 | **cleped** called |
| 105-6 | **Curteys ... so faire** she was courteous, wise, pleasant and friendly, and behaved herself so graciously |
| 108 | **in hoold** in her possession |
| 109 | **loken in every lith** strongly bound in every limb |
| 110 | **He loved ... therwith** he loved her so much that he was truly happy |

*The widow's cockerel, Chauntecleer, is described in magnificent detail. (The realism of the description has led to the identification of his breed as possibly the Golden Spangled Hamburg.) He has the companionship of seven hens, of which his favourite is Pertelote.*

A yeerd she hadde, enclosed al aboute
With stikkes, and a drye dich withoute,
In which she hadde a cok, hight Chauntecleer.
In al the land, of crowing nas his peer.
His voys was murier than the murie orgon      85
On messe-dayes that in the chirche gon.
Wel sikerer was his crowing in his logge
Than is a clokke or an abbey orlogge.
By nature he knew ech ascencioun
Of the equinoxial in thilke toun;      90
For whan degrees fiftene weren ascended,
Thanne crew he, that it mighte nat been amended.
His coomb was redder than the fyn coral,
And batailled as it were a castel wal;
His byle was blak, and as the jeet it shoon;      95
Lyk asure were his legges and his toon;
His nailes whitter than the lilie flour,
And lyk the burned gold was his colour.
This gentil cok hadde in his governaunce
Sevene hennes for to doon al his plesaunce,      100
Whiche were his sustres and his paramours,
And wonder lyk to him, as of colours;
Of whiche the faireste hewed on hir throte
Was cleped faire Damoisele Pertelote.
Curteys she was, discreet, and debonaire,      105
And compaignable, and bar hirself so faire,
Sin thilke day that she was seven night oold,
That trewely she hath the herte in hoold
Of Chauntecleer, loken in every lith;
He loved hire so that wel was him therwith.      110

Chauntecleer's nightmare is experienced at dawn, a time thought by some medieval scholars to indicate that a dream was prophetic. (See page 32 for information on types of dreams.) He describes the frightening fox in detail but, safe inside the yard, has obviously never seen one in real life. His terror would be unsurprising to Chaucer's audience who believed that an animal's fear of its predators was instinctive, not learned through experience.

Beast fables, in which animals behave in some ways like humans and in some ways like themselves, have been popular in most societies since very early times.

- Compare the relationship between Chauntecleer and Pertelote described in lines 105-110 with that revealed by their exchange in lines 123-41. How would you describe the differences?
- The long digression ending on line 405 includes much discussion on the significance of dreams. What other areas of life are touched on?

| | |
|---|---|
| 111 | **hem** them |
| 112 | **gan to springe** began to rise |
| 113 | **accord** harmony |
| | **'My lief is faren in londe!'** 'My love has gone away' [a popular song of the time] |
| 114-5 | **For thilke ... and singe** For at that time, as I understand it, beasts and birds could speak and sing. [Chaucer suggests that animals and birds share with humans not only this ability but also that of experiencing prophetic dreams.] |
| 116 | **bifel** it happened |
| 121 | **drecched** distressed |
| | **soore** severely |
| 123 | **agast** frightened |
| 124 | **eyleth** ails, upsets |
| 125 | **verray** fine [Her tone is ironic.] |

| | |
|---|---|
| 127 | **ye take it nat agrief** don't upset yourself |
| 128 | **me mette I was in swich meschief** I dreamt I was in such misfortune |
| 130 | **my swevene recche aright** interpret my dream favourably [Chaucer often uses the device of dreams, both as a frame for his story, for example in *The Parliament of Fowls*, and as a way of advancing the narrative, as in The Wife of Bath's Tale.] |
| 132 | **me mette** I dreamed [The impersonal form of the verb is used here, and in line 128.] |
| 134 | **wolde han maad areest** wanted to lay hold |
| 137 | **eeris** ears |
| 138 | **smal** narrow |

*One morning Chauntecleer screams out because he is having a terrible dream about a hound-like beast, coloured red and yellow and with black-tipped tail and ears. The creature tried to catch and kill the cockerel. The Tale proper now starts. This section includes a long digression which does not finish until line 405.*

But swich a joye was it to here hem singe,
Whan that the brighte sonne gan to springe,
In sweete accord, 'My lief is faren in londe!'
For thilke time, as I have understonde,
Beestes and briddes koude speke and singe.          115
   And so bifel that in a daweninge,
As Chauntecleer among his wives alle
Sat on his perche, that was in the halle,
And next him sat this faire Pertelote,
This Chauntecleer gan gronen in his throte,          120
As man that in his dreem is drecched soore.
And whan that Pertelote thus herde him roore,
She was agast, and seyde, 'Herte deere,
What eyleth yow, to grone in this manere?
Ye been a verray sleper; fy, for shame.'            125
   And he answerde, and seyde thus: 'Madame,
I pray yow that ye take it nat agrief.
By God, me mette I was in swich meschief
Right now, that yet myn herte is soore afright.
Now God,' quod he, 'my swevene recche aright,        130
And kepe my body out of foul prisoun.
Me mette how that I romed up and doun
Withinne our yeerd, wheer as I saugh a beest
Was lyk an hound, and wolde han maad areest
Upon my body, and wolde han had me deed.            135
His colour was bitwixe yelow and reed,
And tipped was his tail and bothe his eeris
With blak, unlyk the remenant of his heeris;
His snowte smal, with glowinge eyen tweye.
Yet of his look for feere almoost I deye;            140
This caused me my groning, doutelees.'

Medieval doctors believed that health was a matter of balance in the body. All matter depended on two pairs of contraries – Hot and Cold: Dry and Moist. In combination these produced the four elements: Earth, Air, Fire and Water.

Cold and Dry = Earth      Hot and Moist = Air

Hot and Dry = Fire      Cold and Moist = Water

In the human body, the contraries combine to form the Humours:

Cold and Dry = Melancholy      Hot and Moist = Blood

Hot and Dry = Choler      Cold and Moist = Phlegm

The physical characteristics of a person, for example the colour of hair and face, arose from the balance of elements in the body. Humours were also associated with bodily fluids such as blood. Doctors tried to re-balance any excess or deficiency of a bodily fluid – for example by bleeding a sick person.

| FLUID | ELEMENT | HUMOUR | TEMPERAMENT | DESCRIPTION |
|---|---|---|---|---|
| black bile | Earth | Melancholy | melancholic | gloomy, sullen |
| blood | Air | Blood | sanguine | brave, hopeful, |
| red/yellow bile | Fire | Choler | choleric | thin, quarrelsome |
| phlegm | Water | Phlegm | phlegmatic | calm, dull |

• Pertelote has moved from the 'curteys' wife of line 106 to one who can attack her husband at great length. (When she speaks of his lack of a brave and manly heart (line 154), her reference to his beard is particularly appropriate since cockerels of this breed have a 'beard' of feathers at their necks.) Try various ways of delivering lines 142-73 to a partner, perhaps raging – or despairing. Which tone would be the most effective in persuading Chauntecleer to take her advice?

142   **Avoy** alas **herteless** coward

148   **hardy** brave

    **free** generous [This word is linked to the concept of gentillesse and implies a lack of selfishness. In an earlier sense, the word refers to the status of a freeman, as opposed to a serf. There is a certain irony in using the word about chickens which are owned by the Widow.]

149   **secree** discreet **no nigard** not a miser

150   **agast** frightened

    **tool** weapon

151   **avauntour** boaster ['Secree' and 'avauntour' both remind men in the audience to keep quiet about their female conquests, but it is perhaps surprising to find this required in a husband, as well as in a lover.]

152   **dorste** dare

156   **vanitee** emptiness, illusion

158   **fume** vapours rising from the stomach (wind)

159   **complecciouns** temperaments [We still use the word complexion in this sense.]

164   **arwes** arrows **lemes** flames

166   **contek** strife **whelpes** dogs

169   **blake beres, or boles** black bears or bulls

172   **That ... ful wo** that cause many sleepers great distress

173   **lightly** quickly, easily

*Pertelote attacks Chauntecleer's terror at a mere dream; she cannot love a coward. She says that bad dreams result from an imbalance of the bodily humours.*

'Avoy,' quod she, 'fy on yow, hertelees,
Allas,' quod she, 'for, by that God above,
Now han ye lost myn herte and al my love.
I kan nat love a coward, by my feith.          145
For certes, what so any womman seith,
We alle desiren, if it mighte bee,
To han housbondes hardy, wise, and free,
And secree, and no nigard, ne no fool,
Ne him that is agast of every tool,          150
Ne noon avauntour, by that God above.
How dorste ye seyn, for shame, unto youre love
That any thing mighte make yow aferd?
Have ye no mannes herte, and han a berd?
Allas, and konne ye been agast of swevenis?          155
Nothing, God woot, but vanitee in sweven is.
Swevenes engendren of replecciouns,
And ofte of fume and of complecciouns,
Whan humours been to habundant in a wight.
Certes this dreem, which ye han met to-night,          160
Cometh of the greete superfluitee
Of youre rede colera, pardee,
Which causeth folk to dreden in hir dremes
Of arwes, and of fyr with rede lemes,
Of rede beestes, that they wol hem bite,          165
Of contek, and of whelpes, grete and lite;
Right as the humour of malencolie
Causeth ful many a man in sleep to crie
For feere of blake beres, or boles blake,
Or elles blake develes wole hem take.          170
Of othere humours koude I telle also
That werken many a man sleep ful wo;
But I wol passe as lightly as I kan.

Pertelote obviously has an extremely wide knowledge of medicinal herbs and where to find them growing. All the herbs she lists (lawriol/spurge laurel; centaure/centaury; fumetere/fumitory; eelebor/hellebore; katapuce/catapuce; gaitris berys/ buckthorn berries; and ivy) were used by medieval herbalists to treat stomach disorders. Earthworms were sometimes used to treat tertian fever, and of course are part of a chicken's normal diet.

- Discuss with a partner whether or not you agree that dreams can foretell events. Even today people argue about this topic. You may have had personal experience of dreams that came true.
- Pertelote is giving advice, trying to convince Chauntecleer. What are her methods and arguments? Look carefully at the detail and consider her tone. Bossy? Helpful? Does the term 'hen-pecked' have a place here?

| | |
|---|---|
| 174 | **Catoun** Dionysius Cato [the supposed author of *Disticha Catonis*, a collection of Latin sayings. The book was written in the third or fourth century and was widely read in the Middle Ages.] |
| 175 | **Ne do no fors** Take no notice of |
| 176 | **flee fro the bemes** fly down from our perches (beams) |
| 177 | **as taak** please take |
| 179 | **conseille** advise |
| 181 | **for ye shal nat tarie** so you won't delay |
| 184 | **for youre hele and for youre prow** for your health and benefit |
| 186 | **of hire propretee by kinde** the natural properties |
| 187 | **To purge ... above** to make you defecate and also vomit |
| 190 | **Ware** beware |
| 191 | **repleet** full |
| 192 | **leye a grote** bet four pence [the cost of a roast chicken] |
| 193 | **fevere terciane** fever which recurs every other day [and associated particularly with red and black bile] |
| 194 | **agu** acute fever |

| | |
|---|---|
| | **bane** death |
| 200 | **mery is** looks so pleasant |
| 202 | **for youre fader kin** for the sake of your father's family |

*The herb centaury is said to have been discovered by the centaur Chiron*

*Pertelote refers to a medieval school book* Disticha Catonis *to strengthen her argument against believing in dreams. She suggests that as the balance of humours in Chauntecleer is disturbed he should eat a digestive of worms (to absorb melancholy and choler), followed by various laxative herbs.*

---

    Lo Catoun, which that was so wys a man,
Seyde he nat thus, "Ne do no fors of dremes?"        175
Now sire,' quod she, 'whan we flee fro the bemes,
For Goddes love, as taak som laxatif.
Up peril of my soule and of my lyf,
I conseille yow the beste, I wol nat lie,
That bothe of colere and of malencolie        180
Ye purge yow; and for ye shal nat tarie,
Though in this toun is noon apothecarie,
I shal myself to herbes techen yow
That shul been for youre hele and for youre prow;
And in oure yeerd tho herbes shal I finde        185
The whiche han of hire propretee by kinde
To purge yow bynethe and eek above.
Foryet nat this, for Goddes owene love.
Ye been ful colerik of compleccioun;
Ware the sonne in his ascencioun        190
Ne finde yow nat repleet of humours hoote.
And if it do, I dar wel leye a grote,
That ye shul have a fevere terciane,
Or an agu, that may be youre bane.
A day or two ye shul have digestives        195
Of wormes, er ye take youre laxatives
Of lawriol, centaure, and fumetere,
Or elles of ellebor, that groweth there,
Of katapuce, or of gaitris beryis,
Of herbe ive, growing in oure yeerd, ther mery is;        200
Pekke hem up right as they growe and ete hem in.
Be myrie, housbonde, for youre fader kin!
Dredeth no dreem, I kan sey yow namoore.'

Standards of inn varied widely. You could claim the title of 'hostelry' simply by having one spare bed in your house for visitors. In many guest-houses, visitors had to bring and prepare their own meals. Commercial guest-houses, with a regular stream of visitors, were found in towns and ports and on pilgrimage routes. Pressure on space was often intense, as the two pilgrims in Chauntecleer's story find. Beds were usually for at least two guests, often more – even ten. This was quite acceptable and, as people generally slept naked, provided welcome warmth. In 1385 one guest-house in Italy put up 180 people over nineteen days, using four beds and a mattress. The Tabard Inn where Chaucer's pilgrims stayed, offered good accommodation and is praised in The General Prologue. Other types of hospitality were offered by religious houses.

*'ech of hem gooth to his hostelrye'*

- What picture of Chauntecleer is being presented in the conversation so far? Note the tone in lines 204-17. How effective do you find his response to Pertelote?

| | | | |
|---|---|---|---|
| 204 | **graunt mercy of youre loore** many thanks for your teaching | 224 | **o** one/a |
| 206 | **renoun** reputation | 225 | **ylogged** lodged |
| 210 | **so moot I thee** as I hope to prosper | 227 | **departen** part |
| 211 | **That al ... sentence** who say just the opposite of this opinion | 229 | **as it wolde falle** as chance would have it |
| 212 | **significaciouns** signs | 230 | **stalle** stall, stable |
| 216-7 | **Ther nedeth ... in dede** It is unnecessary to put forward supporting arguments; ample proof is shown by what happens | 231 | **Fer in a yeerd** a fair way down the yard |
| | | 233 | **aventure** luck |
| 219 | **whilom** once | 234 | **That us governeth alle as in commune** that controls all of us alike [Chaucer introduces the topic of chance or predestination, which will grow in importance in the Tale.] |
| 220 | **in ful good entente** with most holy intentions | | |
| 222 | **streit of herbergage** shortage of accommodation | | |

*Chauntecleer responds to Pertelote's display of learning by saying that many other authorities believe dreams are prophetic. He begins a tale of two friends on pilgrimage who arrive in a town which is so busy that they are unable to find lodgings together. One stays in a room in a hostelry, the other in the stable attached to another inn.*

'Madame,' quod he, 'graunt mercy of your loore.
But nathelees, as touching Daun Catoun,                          205
That hath of wisdom swich a greet renoun,
Though that he bad no dremes for to drede,
By God, men may in olde bookes rede
Or many a man moore of auctorite
Than evere Caton was, so moot I thee,                           210
That al the revers seyn of this sentence,
And han wel founden by experience
That dremes been significaciouns
As wel of joye as tribulaciouns
That folk enduren in this lif present.                          215
Ther nedeth make of this noon argument;
The verray preeve sheweth it in dede.
    Oon of the gretteste auctour that men rede
Seith thus: that whilom two felawes wente
On pilgrimage, in a ful good entente;                           220
And happed so, they coomen in a toun
Wher as ther was swich congregacioun
Of peple, and eek so streit of herbergage,
That they ne founde as muche as o cotage
In which they bothe mighte ylogged bee.                         225
Wherfore they mosten of necessitee,
As for that night, departen compaignye;
And ech of hem gooth to his hostelrye,
And took his logging as it wolde falle.
That oon of hem was logged in a stalle,                         230
Fer in a yeerd, with oxen of the plough;
That oother man was logged wel ynough,
As was his aventure or his fortune,
That us governeth alle as in commune.

Travel in the Middle Ages was hazardous. In 1286 the Danish King Eric V had been unable to find an inn and was murdered in the barn where he had to sleep.

- Read aloud the lines on the page opposite and compare their flow with that of lines 204-17. It will help to observe the punctuation. What differences do you note, and how do these differences relate to the meaning of the lines?
- What is the effect of repeating the dream three times in Chauntecleer's exemplum? (An exemplum was a rhetorical device often used in disputes. See page 76 for information about rhetoric.) How far do you think it reinforces the moral point?
- Working as a group, put together a list of important aspects of medieval life (for example, religious beliefs, farming) and, as you read the Tale, note examples of each.

| | | | | |
|---|---|---|---|---|
| 242 | **for feere abrayde** in fear, suddenly woke up | | 254 | **Do thilke ... boldely** have that cart seized at once |
| 244 | **took of this no keep** paid no attention to it | | 257 | **hewe** colour (complexion) |
| | | | 260 | **in** inn |
| 245 | **nas but a vanitee** nothing but an empty illusion | | 264 | **is agon** has gone [The innkeeper could be making a black joke here, as the words can also mean 'departed this life'.] |
| 248 | **slawe** slain, murdered | | | |
| 250 | **morwe tide** morning time | | | |
| 253 | **prively** secretly | | | |

*The man in the hostelry twice dreams that his friend has called for help, saying that he is going to be murdered in the stable. The third time he says that he has been murdered for his money, and his body hidden in a dung cart. When the pilgrim makes enquiries, the innkeeper tells him his friend left town at daybreak.*

And so bifel that, longe er it were day,                    235
This man mette in his bed, ther as he lay,
How that his felawe gan upon him calle,
And seyde, "Allas, for in an oxes stalle
This night I shal be mordred ther I lie.
Now help me, deere brother, or I die.                      240
In alle haste com to me," he saide.
This man out of his sleep for feere abrayde;
But whan that he was wakened of his sleep,
He turned him, and took of this no keep.
Him thoughte his dreem nas but a vanitee.                  245
Thus twies in his sleping dremed hee;
And atte thridde time yet his felawe
Cam, as him thoughte, and seide, "I am now slawe.
Bihoold my bloody woundes depe and wide.
Aris up erly in the morwe tide,                            250
And at the west gate of the toun," quod he,
"A carte ful of dong ther shaltow se,
In which my body is hid ful prively;
Do thilke carte arresten boldely.
My gold caused my mordre, sooth to sayn."                  255
And tolde him every point how he was slain,
With a ful pitous face, pale of hewe.
And truste wel, his dreem he foond ful trewe,
For on the morwe, as soone as it was day,
To his felawes in he took the way;                         260
And whan that he cam to this oxes stalle,
After his felawe he bigan to calle.
    The hostiler answerede him anon,
And seyde, "Sire, your felawe is agon.
As soone as day he wente out of the toun."                 265

- There are four chief voices in the Nun's Priest's Tale: Chaucer the author, Chaucer the pilgrim, the Priest and Chauntecleer. Look closely at lines 284-91 and decide whose strongly-held opinion is expressed here.

| | | | |
|---|---|---|---|
| 266 | **gan fallen in suspecioun** became suspicious | 285 | **biwreyest** reveal |
| 268 | **lette** delay | 286 | **Mordre wol out** murder will out [This proverb occurs in The Prioress's Tale, when a body is thrown into a dung-pit.] |
| 270 | **wente as it were to donge lond** gone as if to fertilise the land | | |
| 271 | **arrayed in that same wise** arranged in the precise way | 287 | **wlatsom and abhominable** disgusting and unnatural |
| 272 | **devise** describe | 289 | **heled** concealed |
| 273 | **with an hardy herte** resolutely | 293 | **hent** seized |
| 276 | **lith gaping upright** lies on his back with his mouth open | | **pined** tortured |
| 277 | **ministres** magistrates | 294 | **engined** racked [The rack was a common medieval torture where the body was stretched until a confession was obtained.] |
| 279 | **Harrow** help! | | |
| 281 | **out sterte** leapt into action | | |
| 283 | **al newe** very recently | 295 | **biknewe** confessed |

*Recalling his dream, the traveller finds the dung cart and his murdered friend within. Both the carter and the innkeeper are tortured until they confess, and then hanged.*

---

This man gan fallen in suspecioun,
Remembringe on his dremes that he mette,
And forth he gooth—no lenger wolde he lette—
Unto the west gate of the toun, and fond
A dong-carte, wente as it were to donge lond,        270
That was arrayed in that same wise
As ye han herd the dede man devise.
And with an hardy herte he gan to crye
Vengeance and justice of this felonye.
"My felawe mordred is this same night,        275
And in this carte he lith gaping upright.
I crye out on the ministres," quod he,
"That sholden kepe and reulen this citee.
Harrow, allas, heere lith my felawe slain."
What sholde I moore unto this tale sayn?        280
The peple out sterte and caste the cart to grounde,
And in the middel of the dong they founde
The dede man, that mordred was al newe.
    O blisful God, that art so just and trewe,
Lo, how that thou biwreyest mordre alway.        285
Mordre wol out, that se we day by day.
Mordre is so wlatsom and abhominable
To God, that is so just and resonable,
That he ne wol nat suffre it heled be,
Though it abide a yeer, or two, or thre.        290
Mordre wol out, this my conclusioun.
And right anon, ministres of that toun
Han hent the carter and so soore him pined,
And eek the hostiler so soore engined,
That they biknewe hire wikkednesse anon,        295
And were anhanged by the nekke-bon.

- Medieval belief put dreams into categories. As you read through the Tale, use these categories to classify the nine dreams described or mentioned. Any dream can include elements of more than one type.

**Somnium:** foretells the future in a symbolic way. For example, an egg timer running out might stand for death.

**Insomnium:** does not foretell the future. It is about the dreamer's current preoccupations in life and can be caused by mental distress or physical reasons, such as overworking or overeating.

**Visio:** foretells the future exactly as it will happen.

**Oraculum:** foretells the future through a figure in the dream who describes an event and can advise the sleeper how to avoid it.

**Visum:** does not foretell the future. It occurs when sleepers are only half asleep and think they are still awake. Sleepers see shapes rushing around. Nightmares could come into this category.

- This is obviously the beginning of a highly dramatic exemplum. In a small group discuss how Chaucer's language enhances the drama and urgency in the story.

| | | | |
|---|---|---|---|
| 297 | **been to drede** should be feared | | **fil** befell |
| 300 | **I gabbe ... blis** I do not lie, as I hope for happiness in heaven | | **mervaille** something wonderful |
| | | 312 | **again the day** just before dawn [Chauntecleer's own warning dream occurs at a similar time – line 116.] |
| 303 | **contrarie** against them | | |
| 304-5 | **in a citee ... haven-side** wait in a city situated most pleasantly by the harbour shore | 314 | **abide** remain |
| | | 315 | **wende** depart |
| 306 | **again the even-tide** towards evening | 316 | **dreynt** drowned |
| 307 | **right as hem leste** just as they wanted | 318-9 | **preyde him ... that day** begged him to delay his voyage just for that day |
| 308 | **jolif** cheerful | | |
| 309 | **casten hem** they planned | 321 | **scorned him ful faste** poured great scorn on him |
| 310 | **o** one | | |

*Chauntecleer begins his second example about dreams that warn of disaster. Two men are waiting to take a sea voyage. When the wind eventually becomes favourable they decide to make an early morning start. One of them dreams that if he sails next day he will be drowned. When he tells his friend, the other man laughs at him.*

---

Heere may men seen that dremes been to drede.
And certes in the same book I rede,
Right in the nexte chapitre after this—
I gabbe nat, so have I joye or blis—                                  300
Two men that wolde han passed over see,
For certeyn cause, into a fer contree,
If that the wind ne hadde been contrarie,
That made hem in a citee for to tarie
That stood ful myrie upon an haven-side;                             305
But on a day, again the even-tide,
The wind gan chaunge, and blew right as hem leste.
Jolif and glad they wente unto hir reste,
And casten hem ful erly for to saille.
But to that o man fil a greet mervaille:                             310
That oon of hem, in sleping as he lay,
Him mette a wonder dreem again the day.
Him thoughte a man stood by his beddes side,
And him comanded that he sholde abide,
And sede him thus: "If thou tomorwe wende,                          315
Thow shalt be dreynt; my tale is at an ende."
He wook, and tolde his felawe what he mette,
And preyde him his viage for to lette;
As for that day, he preyde him to bide.
His felawe, that lay by his beddes side,                             320
Gan for to laughe, and scorned him ful faste.

The exact cause of the damage to the ship is not described. The significance of the disaster is that it is fate's doing, indicated by the words 'mischaunce' and 'casuelly'. Look back at page 12 to remind yourself of the importance of this concept in the Tale.

- Try a piece of creative writing – in verse or prose – where a warning dream is ignored or heeded. Chauntecleer's story suggests that what is predicted can be avoided.

| | |
|---|---|
| 322 | **so myn herte agaste** frighten me so much |
| 323 | **That I ... my thinges** that I will neglect my affairs |
| 324 | **sette nat a straw** set no store at all |
| 325 | **vanitees and japes** empty illusions and tricks |
| 326 | **alday** continually [The owl, a night bird, has long been associated with evil. It is not clear why Chaucer includes apes here. It may be that they were also seen as creatures of bad fortune, or it may simply be that they were a convenient rhyme for 'japes'.] |

| | |
|---|---|
| 327 | **maze** delusion |
| 330 | **forslewthen** waste through sloth (idleness) |
| | **tide** time |
| 331 | **God woot, it reweth me** God knows it upsets me |
| 334 | **Noot I ... eyled** I have no idea why, or what misfortune it suffered [Note the use of the double negative.] |
| 340 | **maistow leere** may you learn [**maistow** – mayest thou] |
| 341 | **to recchelees** too heedless |

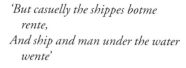

*'But casuelly the shippes botme rente,*
*And ship and man under the water wente'*

*The friend says he has no belief in dreams; they are illusions. He regrets his companion is staying behind wasting time, and leaves on his trip. Before he is halfway through his voyage, the bottom of the ship is smashed in. The man goes down with the ship, in sight of others which had sailed at the same time. Chauntecleer repeats his warnings about dreams to Pertelote.*

---

"No dreem," quod he, "may so myn herte agaste  
That I wol lette for to do my thinges,  
I sette nat a straw by thy dreminges,  
For swevenes been but vanitees and japes,         325  
Men dreme alday of owles and of apes,  
And eek of many a maze therwithal;  
Men dreme of thing that nevere was ne shal.  
But sith I see that thou wolt heere abide,  
And thus forslewthen wilfully thy tide,         330  
God woot, it reweth me; and have good day."  
And thus he took his leve, and wente his way.  
But er that he hadde half his cours yseyled,  
Noot I nat why, ne what mischaunce it eyled,  
But casuelly the shippes botme rente,         335  
And ship and man under the water wente  
In sighte of othere shippes it biside,  
That with hem seyled at the same tide.  
And therfore, faire Pertelote so deere,  
By swiche ensamples olde maistow leere         340  
That no man sholde been to recchelees  
Of dremes; for I seye thee, doutelees,  
That many a dreem ful soore is for to drede.

The feast of the martyr St Kenelm was kept in many churches in the Middle Ages. It was believed that Kenelphus, the King of Mercia, died in 821, to be succeeded by his seven year old son, Kenelm. The boy's ambitious older sister had him killed. Just before the murder he had dreamed of climbing to the top of a tree which had been cut down by his best friend. He had then flown to heaven as a bird. His nurse had warned him this was a prophecy. Some scholars suggest that in fact Kenelm may have died before his father, in battle.

- Chauntecleer has a very wide knowledge of people's experience of dreams. What is your reaction to his apparent learning?
- The Kenelm dream (lines 344-55) is dealt with very differently from the others. Suggest what Chaucer is doing here.

| | | |
|---|---|---|
| 346 | **Mercenrike** Mercia | |
| 347 | **a lite** shortly | |
| 348 | **avisioun** dream of the future | |
| | **say** saw | |
| 349 | **norice** nurse | |
| | **expowned** interpreted | |
| | **deel** part | |
| 350 | **kepe him weel** keep a careful watch out | |
| 351 | **For traisoun** to prevent treachery | |
| | **nas but** was only | |
| 352 | **litel tale hath he toold** attached little importance | |
| 353 | **so hooly was his herte** his heart was so pure | |
| 354 | **levere** rather [Chauntecleer would give up his shirt for Pertelote to have been able to read this story for herself.] | |
| 357 | **Macrobeus** Macrobius [He was a fifth century scholar who wrote a commentary on the dream of Cipioun (Scipio Africanus Minor, a Roman general). Cicero, a Roman orator, in his work, *On the Republic*, | |

included the fictional *Somnium Scipionis* which described a dream apparently experienced by Scipio's grandfather, foretelling that Scipio would destroy Carthage. Macrobius' commentary included a classification of dreams. See page 32 for notes on this.]

| | |
|---|---|
| 362 | **Daniel** [The dreams referred to here can be found in the Old Testament in Daniel chapter 2 verses 31-46 and chapters 4, 7-8 and 10.] |
| 364-9 | [Accounts of the dreams referred to in these lines can be found in Genesis chapter 37 verses 5-10; chapter 40 verses 1-23; chapter 41 verses 1-56.] |
| 365 | **wher** whether |
| 369 | **felte noon effect in dremes** experienced no fulfilment of their dreams |
| 370 | **Whoso ... remes** Whoever wishes to search through the significant events of various countries |
| 372 | **Cresus** King Croesus [This was the last story told by the Monk, about the King of Lydia whose pride prevented him from taking note of his dream and thereby avoiding execution.] |

*Chauntecleer gives several more examples of warning dreams, from history and from the Bible.*

Lo, in the lyf of Seint Kenelm I rede,
That was Kenulphus sone, the noble king                    345
Of Mercenrike, how Kenelm mette a thing.
A lite er he was mordred, on a day,
His mordre in his avisioun he say.
His norice him expowned every deel
His sweven, and bad him for to kepe him weel               350
For traisoun; but he nas but seven yeer oold,
And therfore litel tale hath he toold
Of any dreem, so hooly was his herte.
By God, I hadde levere than my sherte
That ye hadde rad his legende, as have I.                  355
   Dame Pertelote, I sey yow trewely,
Macrobeus, that writ the avisioun
In Affrike of the worthy Cipioun,
Affermeth dremes, and seith that they been
Warninge of thinges that men after seen.                   360
And forthermoore, I pray yow, looketh wel
In the Olde Testament, of Daniel,
If he heeld dremes any vanitee.
Reed eek of Joseph, and ther shul ye see
Wher dremes be somtime—I sey nat alle—                     365
Warninge of thinges that shul after falle.
Looke of Egipte the king, Daun Pharao,
His bakere and his butiller also,
Wher they ne felte noon effect in dremes.
Whoso wol seken actes of sondry remes                      370
May rede of dremes many a wonder thing.
Lo Cresus, which that was of Lyde king,
Mette he nat that he sat upon a tree,
Which signified he sholde anhanged bee?

- Having spent a great deal of time in trying to prove to Pertelote that his dream could be prophetic, Chauntecleer then decides to reject its warning. Why does he do this? In most of the examples he quotes the dreams are similarly ignored. What does this suggest about 'free will'? (See page 44.)
- Apparently in full flow, Chauntecleer suddenly stops his story-telling without going into the details of Hector's death: 'But thilke tale is al to longe to telle,' 'Now let us speke of mirthe' reminds us of the Knight's interruption of the Monk's tediousness. Consider the probable reaction of Pertelote to the stories and also that of the pilgrims to this long digression from the main plotline.
- Having rejected Pertelote's advice about laxatives, Chauntecleer tries to sweeten her through flattery, by praising her appearance, and by mistranslating a Latin saying. 'Mulier est hominis confusio' actually means woman is man's ruin – not his happiness and joy. But, if you think about the story of Adam and Eve, both translations apply. Adam loved Eve, but accepting the apple from her caused them both to be thrown out of the Garden of Eden. Is the Nun's Priest preaching to the pilgrims generally, or is he using the opportunity to have a sly dig at the Prioress?

| | | | |
|---|---|---|---|
| 375 | **Andromacha, Ectores wyf** Andromache, Hector's wife [Hector was a Trojan prince killed by the Greek Achilles in a battle during the Trojan War.] | 390 | **I hem diffye ... deel** I defy them. I don't like them at all |
| 378 | **lorn** lost | 392 | **so have I blis** as I hope to be blessed |
| 384 | **ny day** nearly day | 393 | **large grace** great favour |
| 388 | **ne telle/no stoor** set no store by/have no faith in [Note the double negative.] | 396 | **It maketh ... to dien** it kills all my fear |
| | | 399 | **sentence** meaning |
| | | 402 | **Al be** although |
| | | | **ride** mount |
| | | 404 | **solas** solace, delight |

*Joseph dreamed that in the field his brothers' sheaves bowed down before his sheaf. This caused great jealousy in his brothers*

*Chauntecleer's final example is the death of Hector at the hand of Achilles during the Trojan War; Hector had ignored the warning in a dream experienced by his wife Andromache. The sight of beautiful Pertelote so cheers Chauntecleer that he resolves to ignore his own dream.*

| | |
|---|---:|
| Lo heere Andromacha, Ectores wyf, | 375 |
| That day that Ector sholde lese his lyf, | |
| She dremed on the same night biforn | |
| How that the lyf of Ector sholde be lorn, | |
| If thilke day he wente into bataille. | |
| She warned him, but it mighte nat availle; | 380 |
| He wente for to fighte natheles, | |
| But he was slain anon of Achilles. | |
| But thilke tale is al to longe to telle, | |
| And eek it is ny day, I may nat dwelle. | |
| Shortly I seye, as for conclusioun, | 385 |
| That I shal han of this avisioun | |
| Adversitee; and I seye forthermoor, | |
| That I ne telle of laxatives no stoor, | |
| For they been venymous, I wont it weel; | |
| I hem diffye, I love hem never a deel. | 390 |
|   Now let us speke of mirthe, and stinte al this. | |
| Madam Pertelote, so have I blis, | |
| Of o thing God hath sent me large grace; | |
| For whan I se the beautee of youre face, | |
| Ye been so scarlet reed aboute youre yen, | 395 |
| It maketh al my drede for to dien; | |
| For al so siker as *In principio*, | |
| *Mulier est hominis confusio,*— | |
| Madame, the sentence of this Latin is, | |
| "Womman is mannes joye and al his blis." | 400 |
| For whan I feele a-night your softe side, | |
| Al be it that I may nat on yow ride, | |
| For that oure perche is maad so narwe, allas, | |
| I am so ful of joye and of solas, | |
| That I diffye bothe sweven and dreem.' | 405 |

In the Middle Ages astrology and astronomy were treated as much the same. The sky was divided into twelve signs of the zodiac which were used to devise the calendar. The sign under which you were born was said to affect your character, behaviour and fortune. Chauntecleer's adventure begins on 3 May, under the sign of Taurus the bull, one of the most masculine signs and also one of the signs of Venus – most appropriate for this cockerel, surrounded by females.

- What is achieved by the sudden changes of tone – from the telling of warning dreams, to Chauntecleer's extremely vigorous sexual activity, to the picture of him flaunting himself in the farmyard?

- Chauntecleer seems to think of himself as a prince as he struts on tiptoe amongst his hens. His rejection of his frightening dream has given him renewed confidence and his sexual appetite remains strong. What do you think will be the reactions of the various pilgrims to such open descriptions of farmyard behaviour? Select several pilgrims of contrasting types, for example the Prioress, the Host, the Knight, the Monk, and write a few lines indicating their thoughts as they listen.

- On 3 May Chauntecleer is 'in al his pride' (line 425) and of course, everyone knows 'pride comes before a fall'. What methods are used in the lines on the page opposite to emphasise both pride and fall? Note other instances of Chauntecleer's pride as you read on.

| | | | |
|---|---|---|---|
| 408 | **chuk** cluck | 419 | **pasture** feeding [the act of eating, not the ground on which the food grows] |
| 410 | **real** regal | | |
| 411 | **fethered** caressed with his wings | 430 | **kinde** instinct |
| 412 | **trad** copulated with | | **loore** learning |
| 413 | **leoun** lion | 431 | **stevene** voice |
| 415 | **deigned nat** did not deign/condescend | 437 | **revel** revelry, pleasure |

*This sixteenth century calendar clearly shows the twelve signs of the zodiac*

*Since it is daybreak, Chauntecleer and the hens fly down from the beam; he calls to them as he has
found corn in the yard. He copulates with Pertelote twenty times before prime (6 a.m.). He
behaves like a prince amongst his hens. The Nun's Priest sets the scene of Chauntecleer's adventure
with a very detailed calculation of the exact time and date.*

And with that word he fley doun fro the beem,
For it was day, and eke his hennes alle,
And with a chuk he gan hem for to calle,
For he hadde founde a corn, lay in the yerd.
Real he was, he was namoore aferd.                              410
He fethered Pertelote twenty time,
And trad hire eke as ofte, er it was prime.
He looketh as it were a grim leoun,
And on his toos he rometh up and doun;
Him deigned nat to sette his foot to grounde.                   415
He chukketh whan he hath a corn yfounde,
And to him rennen thanne his wives alle.
Thus roial, as a prince is in his halle,
Leve I this Chauntecleer in his pasture,
And after wol I telle his aventure.                             420
  Whan that the month in which the world bigan,
That highte March, whan God first maked man,
Was compleet, and passed were also,
Sin March bigan, thritty dayes and two,
Bifel that Chauntecleer in al his pride,                        425
His sevene wives walkinge by his side,
Caste up his eyen to the brighte sonne,
That in the signe of Taurus hadde yronne
Twenty degrees and oon, and somwhat moore,
And knew by kinde, and by noon oother loore,                   430
That it was prime, and crew with blisful stevene.
'The sonne,' he seyde, 'is clomben up on hevene
Fourty degrees and oon, and moore, ywis.
Madame Pertelote, my worldes blis,
Herkneth thise blisful briddes how they singe,                 435
And se the fresshe floures how they springe;
Ful is myn herte of revel and solas.'

- Lines 438-48 are a conventional sermon, of a sort often inserted in Chaucer's work. What effect do you think it has in altering the narrative, or moving it on?
- The fox is compared to three traitors of whom the Nun's Priest's listeners would often have heard. Judas Iscariot betrayed Jesus to the authorities, leading to His death. Ganelon betrayed Emperor Charlemagne's forces. During the Trojan War the huge wooden Trojan Horse was allowed into Troy on Sinon's advice. It was full of Greek soldiers who crept out in the night and captured the city. The repeated 'O' is a rhetorical device called apostrophe (see page 76). What do you think is the effect of choosing such important figures to compare with a mere fox and cockerel, and of employing such a high flown style?

| 438 | **him fil a sorweful cas** he was overtaken by a lamentable accident |
| 440 | **ago** gone |
| 441-3 | **And if ... notabilitee** If a master of rhetoric could compose well, he could confidently write this down in a history as a most significant observation |
| 446-7 | **Launcelot** [Sir Lancelot is the lover of Queen Guinevere in the story of King Arthur. The Nun's Priest seems to be mocking the women (even the Prioress?) who enjoy such romances, and saying that his tale is just as worthwhile and as true. **That** may refer to Lancelot himself, or to the book.] |
| 449 | **col-fox** fox with coal black markings [See page 71.] |
| 450 | **woned** lived |
| 451 | **By heigh imaginacioun forncast** [**Forncast** means pre-planned or forecast. You could interpret the line as meaning that God had predestined |

the event (see page 44 for notes on predestination) or that Chauntecleer's strong imagination in his dream had foretold what was to happen. The closest modern equivalent is 'with malice aforethought'; there seems to have been a legal as well as a philosophical meaning.]

| 452 | **The same ... brast** the same night of Chauntecleer's dream he burst through the hedges/fences |
| 454 | **Was wont ...to repaire** was in the habit of frequently going |
| 455 | **wortes** vegetables |
| 456 | **undren** [This word changed in meaning during the Middle Ages, to indicate early morning, noon and mid afternoon. Here, it must mean 9 a.m.] |
| 459 | **That in await ... men** That lie in wait to murder people |
| 462 | **dissimulour** deceiver |
| 463 | **outrely** utterly |

*The Priest pauses to make a point about the misfortune that always follows happiness. Returning to his story, he describes a crafty fox which one night breaks into the yard and lies in wait for Chauntecleer in a vegetable bed.*

But sodeynly him fil a sorweful cas,
For evere the latter ende of joye is wo.
God woot that worldly joye is soone ago;                    440
And if a rethor koude faire endite,
He in a cronicle saufly mighte it write
As for a sovereyn notabilitee.
Now every wys man, lat him herkne me;
This storie is also trewe, I undertake,                     445
As is the book of Launcelot de Lake,
That wommen holde in ful greet reverence.
Now wol I torne again to my sentence.
   A col-fox, ful of sly iniquitee,
That in the grove hadde woned yeres three,                  450
By heigh imaginacioun forncast,
The same night thurghout the hegges brast
Into the yerd ther Chauntecleer the faire
Was wont, and eek his wives to repaire;
And in a bed of wortes stille he lay,                       455
Til it was passed undren of the day,
Waitinge his time on Chauntecleer to falle,
As gladly doon thise homicides alle
That in await liggen to mordre men.
O false mordrour, lurkinge in thy den,                      460
O newe Scariot, newe Genilon,
False dissimulour, o Greek Sinon,
That broghtest Troye al outrely to sorwe,
O Chauntecleer, acursed be that morwe
That thou into that yerd flaugh fro the bemes.              465

The Nun's Priest refers to an old debate which had come back with force in the four-teenth century – whether God's foreknowledge ('forwiting') is consistent with human free will. If God knows what is going to happen, is it possible for a human to act freely, without being compelled by God? Most often quoted on the question was St Augustine of Hippo (354-430 CE), who in old age had argued that human free will was essentially illusory, as compared with God's power and knowledge. Chaucer faced the question while translating into English *The Consolation of Philosophy* of Boethius (480-524 CE). Boethius had argued, in modification of Augustine, that just as hindsight cannot alter the way people act, so God's foreknowledge does not affect a person's free will, although God exercises a providential control for good over the sum of human events. Of the English contributors to the 'altercacioun' the most well-known was Thomas Bradwardine (*c.* 1290-1349), who had died during the Black Death while Archbishop of Canterbury. In *De Causa Dei* (The Case for God) he took the same line as Augustine, and answered contemporaries who said it was Man's will, not God's, which determined the course of events.

Chaucer discusses the subject in *Troilus and Criseyde*, Book 4, lines 953-1078. The monk and philosopher William of Occam said that 'laymen and old women' argued about it as heatedly as did academics.

- Discuss why you think Chaucer includes this topic in a farmyard story. Is he suggesting that ordinary people cannot be expected to come to a conclusion when experts disagree ('in scole is greet altercacion') – or is he simply making his audience laugh, by including it in an inappropriate setting?
- What are your views on predestation and free will? How far do you think people's actions are influenced by genetic make-up and by social background?

468     **But what ... bee** but what God has foreknowledge of must necessarily come to pass

474     **But I ne kan ... bren** I am unable to sift it from the bran, I can't get at the core of the discussion on free will

477-8     **Wheither ... thing** whether God's divine foreknowledge must necessarily (**nedely**) constrain me to do something

482     **Though ... wroght** Though God knew of it before it was done [In some editions the word 'it' or 'I' is inserted between 'that' and 'was wroght'. 'I' would give the most all-encom-passing idea – that God knows every-thing before a person is born.]

483     **witing** knowing

    **streyneth** constrains, necessitates

490     **colde** fatal

497     **auctors** authors, authorities

500     **divine** suppose

*'Wommannes conseil broghte us first to wo, And made Adam from Paradis to go'. (Here, even the snake is female.)*

*The Nun's Priest speaks about predestination and of the dire consequences of taking advice from women.*

---

Thou were ful wel ywarned by thy dremes
That thilke day was perilous to thee;
But what that God forwoot moot nedes bee,
After the opinioun of certein clerkis.
Witnesse on him that any parfit clerk is,                  470
That in scole is greet altercacioun
In this mateere, and greet disputisoun,
And hath been of an hundred thousand men.
But I ne kan nat bulte it to the bren
As kan the hooly Doctour Augustin,                          475
Or Boece, or the Bisshop Bradwardin,
Wheither that Goddes worthy forwiting
Streyneth me nedely for to doon a thing,—
'Nedely' clepe I simple necessitee;
Or elles, if free chois be graunted me                     480
To do that same thing, or do it noght,
Though God forwoot it er that was wroght;
Or if his witing streyneth never a deel
But by necessitee condicioneel.
I wol nat han to do of swich mateere;                       485
My tale is of a cok, as ye may heere,
That tok his conseil of his wyf, with sorwe,
To walken in the yerd upon that morwe
That he hadde met that dreem that I yow tolde.
Wommannes conseils been ful ofte colde;                     490
Wommannes conseil broghte us first to wo,
And made Adam fro Paradis to go,
Ther as he was ful myrie and wel at ese.
But for I noot to whom it might displese,
If I conseil of wommen wolde blame,                         495
Passe over, for I seyde it in my game.
Rede auctours, where they trete of swich mateere,
And what they seyn of wommen ye may heere.
Thise been the cokkes wordes, and nat mine;
I kan noon harm of no womman divine.                        500

- The Nun's Priest switches from a deep discussion of predestination and of the Fall of Man to a description of chickens having a dustbath. These sudden changes of tone are typical of his tale. How do they add to our enjoyment of the whole tale?
- 'Gentil sire': Compose a few lines to flatter someone you know, perhaps teacher, parent, friend, employer, in order to achieve what you want.

| | |
|---|---|
| 502 | **lith** lies |
| 503 | **again** in |
| 504 | [Mermaids – women with fish tails – supposedly lured sailors to their deaths by singing. Chauntecleer's singing may lead to his own downfall.] |
| 505 | **Phisiologus** [This refers to a bestiary – or study of animals – well-known in a Latin version in the Middle Ages. It dealt with real creatures, and imaginary ones, such as mermaids.] |
| 510 | **Nothing ne liste ... crowe** he had absolutely no desire to crow at that moment [Note the emphatic double negative.] |
| 513-5 | **For natureelly ... contrarie** [It was believed that everything in the world, both living and inanimate, had its opposite, towards which it felt an instinctive antipathy.] |
| 515 | **erst** before |
| 519 | **feend** devil |
| 521 | **wolde** intended to do |
| | **vileynye** discourtesy [The opposite of the virtues embodied by gentilesse.] |
| 522 | **I am ... t'espye** I have not come to spy on your secret plans |
| 525 | **stevene** voice |
| 528 | **Boece** Boethius [His *De Musica* (On Music) was used for teaching the theory of music in universities, and did not deal with harmonies or the natural music of birds, so the fox's reference to it is really a joke.] |

*Chauntecleer and the hens are enjoying the sun, having a happy dustbath in the sand. While Chauntecleer is singing he notices the fox amongst the vegetables. He is afraid and is about to run away when the fox begins to flatter him by praising his heavenly singing.*

Faire in the soond, to bathe hire myrily,
Lith Pertelote, and alle hire sustres by,
Again the sonne, and Chauntecleer so free
Soong murier than the mermaide in the see;
For Phisiologus seith sikerly                                    505
How that they singen wel and myrily.
And so bifel that, as he caste his ye
Among the wortes on a boterflye,
He was war of this fox, that lay ful lowe.
Nothing ne liste him thanne for to crowe,                        510
But cride anon, 'Cok, cok!' and up he sterte
As man that was affrayed in his herte.
For natureelly a beest desireth flee
Fro his contrarie, if he may it see,
Though he never erst hadde seyn it with his ye.                  515
  This Chauntecleer, whan he gan him espye,
He wolde han fled, but that the fox anon
Seyde, 'Gentil sire, allas, wher wol ye gon?
Be ye affrayed of me that am youre freend?
Now, certes, I were worse than a feend,                          520
If I to yow wolde harm or vileynye,
I am nat come youre conseil for t'espye,
But trewely, the cause of my cominge
Was oonly for to herkne how that ye singe.
For trewely, ye have as myrie a stevene                          525
As any aungel hath that is in hevene.
Therwith ye han in musik moore feelinge
Than hadde Boece, or any that kan singe.

- The fox's speech is a masterpiece of cunning and flattery, perfect for persuading a creature as vain as Chauntecleer to do what the fox wants. Look carefully at the whole speech (from line 518) and note the points which are calculated to please Chauntecleer and calm his fear. Work out what there is in this speech which would indicate to the audience the fox's true purpose.

| | |
|---|---|
| 530 | **hire** their |
| 531 | **to my greet ese** to my great pleasure [The fox's pleasure was to eat the chickens!] |
| 532 | **fain** gladly |
| 533 | **for men speke of singing** as the subject under discussion is singing |
| 534 | **So moote ... tweye** as I hope to use both my eyes well [It is ironic that the fox is about to suggest that Chauntecleer close both his eyes.] |
| 535 | **save** except for |
| 537 | **Certes, it was of herte** certainly it was heartfelt |
| 539 | **so peyne him** take such pains, make such an effort |
| 540 | **He moste winke** he had to keep his eyes closed |
| 541 | **And stonden ... therwithal** and stand on tiptoe as well |
| 543 | **discrecioun** discernment |
| 544 | **That ther nas no man in no regioun** [Note the emphatic triple negative.] |
| 545 | **passe** outdo |

| | |
|---|---|
| 546-50 | [These lines refer to an incident in the poem 'Speculum Stultorum' written in the twelfth century by a monk named Nigellus Wireker. The main character in the poem is Burnellus the little brown ass, but the Nun's Priest is talking about another strand of the story. In this, a young man, Gundolf, broke a cockerel's leg by throwing a stone at it. When he grew up he prepared for the priesthood. On the morning when he was to be ordained the cockerel crowed very late, so that Gundolf overslept, missed the ordination service and lost his benefice.] |
| 549 | **nice** foolish |
| 550 | **benefice** church living, parish |
| 553 | **his subtiltee** [This refers to the ingenuity of the cockerel in not crowing for Gundolf at the right time. Ironically, the fox is suggesting to Chauntecleer that he does the exact opposite, and show off his voice immediately.] |
| 554 | **for seinte charitee** for charity's sake |
| 555 | **Lat se ... countrefete** show me if you can imitate your father |

*The fox recalls the time when Chauntecleer's parents visited his house. He gives a detailed description of the father's voice and of his singing technique. The fox compares the cockerel to one in a famous Latin poem.*

My lord youre fader—God his soule blesse—
And eek youre mooder, of hire gentillesse,                        530
Han in myn hous ybeen to my greet ese;
And certes, sire, ful fain wolde I yow plese.
But, for men speke of singing, I wol seye,—
So moote I brouke wel mine eyen tweye,—
Save yow, I herde nevere man so singe                            535
As dide youre fader in the morweninge.
Certes, it was of herte, al that he song.
And for to make his voys the moore strong,
He wolde so peyne him that with bothe his yen
He moste winke, so loude he wolde cryen,                         540
And stonden on his tiptoon therwithal,
And strecche forth his nekke long and smal.
And eek he was of swich discrecioun
That ther nas no man in no regioun
That him in song or wisedom mighte passe.                        545
I have wel rad in "Daun Burnel the Asse,"
Among his vers, how that ther was a cok,
For that a preestes sone yaf him a knok
Upon his leg whil he was yong and nice,
He made him for to lese his benefice.                            550
But certeyn, ther nis no comparisoun
Betwixe the wisedom and discrecioun
Of youre fader and of his subtiltee.
Now singeth, sire, for seinte charitee;
Lat se, konne ye youre fader countrefete?'                       555

- This section contains three examples of apostrophe (see page 76). They are written in mock-heroic style, for humorous effect. Write your own mock-heroic apostrophe and then read it aloud to your group. The more undeserving the subject, the more amusing the result will be. The subject does not have to be a person, for example: 'O school, wherein I spend my happiest hours!'
- Another way of approaching the mock heroic style would be to deliver this incident to your group in the manner of the chorus of a Greek play.

557 **As man** like someone

**traisoun** betrayal

**espie** see/be aware of

558 **ravisshed with** seduced by

559 **flatour** flatterer

[It is not clear who the 'lordes' are. Perhaps Chaucer the poet is addressing his courtly audience, but possibly the Nun's Priest is adding a little stylistic flourish to his story.]

559-64 [A little sermon, to warn against the treacherous deceiving pleasure of flattery. The Priest may be referring to the book of Ecclesiastes, chapter 12, verse 15: 'An enemy speaketh sweetly with his lips, but in his heart he lieth in wait, to throw thee into a pit,' or possibly to Proverbs, chapter 29, verse 5.]

560 **losengeour** flatterer, deceiver

562 **soothfastnesse** truth

564 **Beth war** be aware

567 **for the nones** for the occasion

568 **atones** at once, immediately

569 **gargat** throat

**hente** grabbed

571 **sewed** chased

572 **eschewed** avoided

574 **roghte** took no warning from

579 [The medieval church taught that sex was a sin unless its only purpose was to conceive children (to 'multiplye'). It was not to be enjoyed (to 'delit'). These lofty ideals are ridiculed by being mentioned in connection with Chauntecleer and his seven lovers – and Venus, a pagan goddess of love.]

580 **woldestow** would you

581-3 **Gaufred** Geoffrey de Vinsauf [See page 76 for information on de Vinsauf and Richard I.]

584 **thy sentence and thy loore** your intelligence and learning

587 **pleyne** lament

*Chauntecleer is taken in by the fox's flattery. There is a brief sermon on human susceptibility to flattery. As soon as Chauntecleer closes his eyes and starts to sing, the fox grabs him and makes off for the wood. The Priest, full of regret for this terrible event, compares it to the death of Richard I, which also occurred on a Friday, recalling the death of Christ on the cross on Good Friday.*

This Chauntecleer his winges gan to bete,
As man that koude his traisoun nat espie,
So was he ravisshed with his flaterie.
   Allas, ye lordes, many a fals flatour
Is in youre courtes, and many a losengeour,                 560
That plesen yow wel moore, by my feith,
Than he that soothfastnesse unto yow seith.
Redeth Ecclesiaste of flaterye;
Beth war, ye lordes, of hir trecherye.
   This Chauntecleer stood hie upon his toos,               565
Strecchinge his nekke, and heeld his eyen cloos,
And gan to crowe loude for the nones.
And Daun Russell the fox stirte up atones,
And by the gargat hente Chauntecleer,
And on his bak toward the wode him beer,                    570
For yet ne was ther no man that him sewed.
   O destinee, that mayst nat been eschewed,
Allas, that Chauntecleer fleigh fro the bemes,
Allas, his wif ne roghte nat of dremes,
And on a Friday fil al this meschaunce!                     575
   O Venus, that art goddesse of plesaunce,
Sin that thy servant was this Chauntecleer,
And in thy service dide al his poweer,
Moore for delit than world to multiplye,
Why woldestow suffre him on thy day to die?                 580
   O Gaufred, deere maister soverain,
That whan thy worthy King Richard was slain
With shot, compleynedest his deeth so soore,
Why ne hadde I now thy sentence and thy loore,
The Friday for to chide, as diden ye?                       585
For on a Friday, soothly, slain was he.
Thanne wolde I shewe yow how that I koude pleyne
For Chauntecleres drede and for his peyne.

- The lamentation of the hens at Chauntecleer's capture is compared to the misery of famous women in dire circumstances. Comparisons were a rhetorical device. It is not surprising that the hens are so distraught about their lover when he is so magnificent. Look back at lines 86-98 to see the same technique used in the description of him. Try reading this section aloud, followed by lines 589-607. What impression does this comparison make on you?
- Decide what difference it makes to your impression that the Nun's Priest returns to the plot of his tale so abruptly, in the middle of a rhyming couplet in line 608.

| | |
|---|---|
| 590-3 | [In Virgil's epic poem *The Aeneid* (**Eneydos**) Troy (**Ilion**) was defeated by the Greeks. Pyrrhus killed the old Trojan king Priam at an altar of Jupiter, and cut off his head.] |
| 591 | **streite swerd** drawn sword |
| 594 | **clos** enclosed yard |
| 596 | **sovereynly** supremely [Perterlote made more noise than Hasdrubal's widow.] |
| | **shrighte** shrieked |

| | |
|---|---|
| 597-602 | [In 146 BCE Carthage was burned down by the Romans during the Punic Wars. Hasdrubal was the Carthaginian leader. His wife threw herself and their sons into the fire.] |
| 599 | **brend** burned |
| 604-7 | [In 46 CE there was a great fire in Rome. It should probably be blamed on the emperor Nero, but he accused the Christians and used it as an excuse to persecute them. The senators whom Nero had killed were innocent – **withouten gilt**.] |

*The Nun's Priest gives examples of extreme reactions by women in classical mythology to the deaths of their husbands. He then returns abruptly to his tale.*

Certes, swich cry ne lamentacion,
Was nevere of ladies maad whan Ilion                    590
Was wonne, and Pirrus with his streite swerd,
Whan he hadde hent King Priam by the berd,
And slain him, as seith us *Eneydos*,
As maden alle the hennes in the clos,
Whan they had seyn of Chauntecleer the sighte.         595
But sovereynly Dame Pertelote shrighte
Ful louder than dide Hasdrubales wyf,
Whan that hir housbonde hadde lost his lyf,
And that the Romayns hadde brend Cartage.
She was so ful of torment and of rage                  600
That wilfully into the fyr she sterte,
And brende hirselven with a stedefast herte.
    O woful hennes, right so criden ye,
As, whan that Nero brende the citee
Of Rome, cryden senatoures wives                        605
For that hir husbondes losten alle hir lives,—
Withouten gilt this Nero hath hem slain.
Now wole I turne to my tale again.

A modern reader might think this is too much fuss over one bird, but the loss of Chauntecleer would have been a considerable financial blow for the poor widow.

- How is the telling of the end of Chauntecleer's adventure made exciting? The audience have been waiting a long time to hear it, so dramatic tension is quite high. Is the wait worth it? Consider, for example, the use of onomatopoeia, alliteration, rhyme and rhythm. Try reading the section aloud and compare it with a reading of a 'quieter' section. You might like to consider how a film director would create an exciting chase sequence.

In 1381 the Peasants' Revolt took place in England. Riots had begun in 1379 over a poll tax. As the revolt spread, other matters of discontent were addressed. In 1381 the rebels sacked Canterbury, then marched to London, where they burnt John of Gaunt's palace, took the Fleet and Newgate prisons and the Tower of London. They beheaded Archbishop Sudbury, the Lord Treasurer, and other officials. Jack Straw was a rebel leader who was hanged. Chaucer was probably in London at the time and it is perhaps surprising that he makes so little reference to these events in his writing, especially as three of his associates helped put down the rising. During the Revolt wealthy Flemish wool-traders in London became a target. Some forty people were dragged out of a church and beheaded, their bodies left in Thames Street, near Chaucer's family home.

- In line 631 the noise of the mob intent on these horrific murders is compared to the noise of the people and animals chasing the fox. What is your response to this comparison?
- At this stage of the beast fable the humans join the action. How important is their arrival?
- In line 609 the widow is described as 'sely'. This word can have many shades of meaning such as: simple, innocent, good, humble, poor, hapless, wretched. Decide which you think is the most appropriate here.

| | |
|---|---|
| 614 | **harrow, and weylaway** help and alas |
| 617 | **Colle ... Talbot and Gerland** [Colle is a rustic name given to a dog; the other two are rather more aristocratic.] |
| 618 | **Malkin** [Probably the widow's name, a form of Mathilda.] |
| | **distaf** a cleft stick used for spinning |
| 619-20 | **eek ... dogges** even the pigs were so frightened because of the dogs' barking |

| | |
|---|---|
| 622 | **They ... breeke** they ran so hard they thought their hearts would break |
| 623 | **yolleden** yelled |
| | **feendes** fiends, devils |
| 624 | **quelle** kill |
| 627 | **a, *benedicitee*** O God bless us |
| 628 | **meynee** followers, the mob |
| 632 | **bemes** trumpets |
| | **box** boxwood |
| 633 | **powped** puffed, blew |
| 634 | **howped** whooped |

*The Nun's Priest picks up his tale almost as if lines 572-608 did not exist. The widow, her daughters, men with sticks, and dogs, begin to chase the fox. The noise frightens all the farmyard creatures, even the bees. They make more noise than Jack Straw and the mob during the Peasants' Revolt.*

This sely widwe and eek hir doghtres two
Herden thise hennes crie and maken wo,                    610
And out at dores stirten they anon,
And syen the fox toward the grove gon,
And bar upon his bak the cok away,
And criden, 'Out, harrow, and weylaway.
Ha, ha, the fox!' and after him they ran,                 615
And eek with staves many another man.
Ran Colle oure dogge, and Talbot and Gerland,
And Malkin, with a distaf in hir hand;
Ran cow and calf, and eek the verray hogges,
So fered for the berking of the dogges                    620
And shouting of the men and wommen eeke,
They ronne so hem thoughte hir herte breeke.
They yolleden as feendes doon in helle;
The dokes cryden as men wolde hem quelle;
The gees for feere flowen over the trees;                 625
Out of the hive cam the swarm of bees.
So hidous was the noise, a, *benedicitee!*
Certes, he Jakke Straw and his meynee
Ne made nevere shoutes half so shrille
Whan that they wolden any Fleming kille,                  630
As thilke day was maad upon the fox.
Of bras they broghten bemes, and of box,
Of horn, of boon, in whiche they blewe and powped,
And therwithal they shriked and they howped.
It seemed as that hevene sholde falle.

- Sermonising again in lines 636-7 the Nun's Priest draws his listeners' attention to the power of Dame Fortune. Having spent so long discussing various theologians' ideas about predestination, why do you think he ends by apparently accepting blind Fortune?
- In pairs or small groups, prepare and act a short scene showing a modern human version of Chauntecleer's encounter with the fox. Remember the main weapon of the predator is flattery, and both animals suffer for their pride. A political theme might be suitable ...

641 **if I were as ye** if I were in your position

642 **Yet ... me** I would say, as surely as God may help me

643 **cherles** fellows

644 **verray pestilence** true plague

646 **maugree youre heed** in spite of anything you can do

650 **brak** escaped

**deliverly** quickly

*'Lo, how Fortune turneth sodeynly'*

*Fortune turns again. Chauntecleer, though frightened, has the idea of suggesting to the fox that he curse the crowd chasing him and tell them they have no chance of rescuing the cockerel. The fox opens his mouth to speak and Chauntecleer escapes to a tree.*

---

Now, goode men, I prey yow herkneth alle:
Lo, how Fortune turneth sodeynly
The hope and pride eek of hir enemy.
This cok, that lay upon the foxes bak,
In al his drede unto the fox he spak,            640
And seyde, 'Sire, if that I were as ye,
Yet sholde I seyn, as wis God helpe me,
"Turneth again, ye proude cherles alle,
A verray pestilence upon yow falle.
Now am I come unto the wodes syde;            645
Maugree youre heed, the cok shal heere abide.
I wol him ete, in feith, and that anon".'
   The fox answerde, 'In feith, it shal be don.'
And as he spak that word, al sodeynly
This cok brak from his mouth deliverly,            650
And heighe upon a tree he fleigh anon.

- Write the account of his adventure which Chauntecleer gives to the hens when they all return to their perch. His story will doubtless be heavily embroidered to show him in a flattering light. You may wish to add the reactions of Pertelote and the other hens.
- In early beast fables, the characters were one-dimensional. Look back over the Tale and consider how the characters of Chauntecleer, Pertelote and Daun Russell the fox have been developed.
- How important a part does the poor widow play in the story? Is she, in her poverty, simply a comical contrast to the resplendent cockerel, or can you find some moral and allegorical significance for her character?
- Discuss with a partner what you think of the value of the moral statements in this final section. Look at lines 661-6; 667-9; 670-1. How effectively does the Tale illustrate these morals?

| | |
|---|---|
| 654 | **ydoon trespas** done an injury |
| 657 | **wikke entente** evil intention |
| 660 | **shrewe** curse |
| 662 | **If ... ones** If you deceive me more than once |
| 666 | **wilfully** voluntarily |
| | **thee** prosper |
| 668 | **undiscreet of governaunce** foolishly lacking in self control |
| 669 | **jangleth** chatters |
| 670 | **recchelees** careless |

| | |
|---|---|
| 672 | **folye** silly thing |
| 674 | **taketh the moralite** take the moral teaching to heart |
| 676 | **To ... ywis** it is certainly written for our guidance |
| 677 | **Taketh ... ne stille** take the important parts (**fruit**) and leave the useless parts (**chaff**) lying there [This is a harvesting metaphor. It could be taken to mean 'Take to heart the meaning of the tale'. The chaff represents the words by which the meaning is expressed.] |

*The fox apologises for frightening Chauntecleer and asks him to come down from the tree for a full explanation. Chauntecleer is not to be deceived twice. The Nun's Priest ends his tale with an indication of the moral of the story.*

And whan the fox saugh that the cok was gon,
  'Allas,' quod he, 'O Chauntecleer, allas,
I have to yow,' quod he, 'ydoon trespas,
In as muche as I maked yow aferd          655
Whan I yow hente and broghte out of the yerd.
But, sire, I dide it in no wikke entente.
Com doun, and I shal telle yow what I mente;
I shal seye sooth to yow, God help me so.'
  'Nay thanne,' quod he, 'I shrewe us bothe two.    660
And first I shrewe myself, bothe blood and bones,
If thou bigile me ofter than ones.
Thou shalt namoore, thurgh thy flaterye,
Do me to singe and winke with myn ye;
For he that winketh, whan he sholde see,     665
Al wilfully, God lat him nevere thee!'
  'Nay,' quod the fox, 'but God yeve him meschaunce,
That is so undiscreet of governaunce
That jangleth whan he sholde holde his pees.'
  Lo, swich it is for to be recchelees      670
And necligent, and truste on flaterye.
  But ye that holden this tale a folye,
As of a fox, or of a cok and hen,
Taketh the moralite, goode men.
For Seint Paul seith that al that writen is,    675
To oure doctrine it is ywrite, ywis;
Taketh the fruit, and lat the chaf be stille.
  Now, goode God, if that it be thy wille,
As seith my lord, so make us alle goode men,
And bringe us to his heighe blisse! Amen.    680

- 'Now, sire, faire falle yow for youre tale!' Write your own critical review of the Nun's Priest's Tale, paying attention to all the elements in it such as plot, morals, humour, digressions. Think particularly of Chaucer's construction of the Tale, given that so little of it is given up to the story of Chauntecleer, and so much to other purposes and effects.
- To whom is the Host addressing his rather crude comments about the Priest's likely sexual vigour? Just the Priest, or would there be other pilgrims who would appreciate his humour? How might the Prioress or the Knight react? In what ways does the Epilogue change your view of the Nun's Priest?

| | | | | |
|---|---|---|---|---|
| 682 | **breche** breeches | | 691 | **sperhauk** sparrowhawk |
| | **stoon** testicle | | | **yen** eyes |
| 684 | **seculer** a layman [Priests were supposed to be celibate.] | | 692 | **Him nedeth ... dyen** he doesn't need to brighten himself up artificially [to make himself sexually attractive] |
| 685 | **trede-foul** lover of hens, lecher | | 693 | **brasile** brazil wood (red) |
| 686 | **corage** sexual vigour | | | **greyn of Portingale** Portuguese cochineal grain [also red] |
| 687 | **as I wene** I would think | | 694 | **faire falle yow** good luck to you |
| 689 | **braunes** muscles/brawn | | | |

*In the Epilogue the Host blesses the Nun's Priest for his cheery tale and suggests he would be more*
*sexually active than Chauntecleer if he were not a priest. He draws attention to the priest's manly*
*appearance and ruddy complexion and wishes him luck.*

---

'Sire Nonnes Preest,' oure Hooste seide anoon,
'I-blessed be thy breche, and every stoon,
This was a murie tale of Chauntecleer.
But by my trouthe, if thou were seculer,
Thou woldest ben a trede-foul aright.    685
For if thou have corage as thou hast might,
Thee were nede of hennes, as I wene,
Ya, moo than seven times seventene.
See, whiche braunes hath this gentil preest,
So gret a nekke, and swich a large breest,   690
He loketh as a sperhauk with his yen;
Him nedeth nat his colour for to dyen
With brasile, ne with greyn of Portingale.
Now, sire, faire falle yow for youre tale!'
 [And after that he, with ful merie chere,   695
Seide unto another, as ye shuln heere.]

# The Prioress, madame Eglentine

There is no description of the Nun's Priest in The General Prologue, but there is one of the Prioress, the head of the convent to which he is attached. This has been included here to help you put him in context. The Priest makes some allusions to the Prioress in his tale. For example, see pages 16-17. His tale concerns the relationship between the sexes, something from which the Prioress is excluded, although the message on her rosary might indicate a not entirely spiritual feeling.

The portrait of the Prioress in The General Prologue is one of the funniest of Chaucer's descriptions. She spends much of her time cultivating what she sees as courtly behaviour – even making sure that she sings in the most attractive and fashionable way she can during the services. Read the description of her and you will find that every time Chaucer pays her a compliment he undermines it in some way. For example, she speaks French – but with an English accent. She is complimented for her lovely forehead – but of course a nun should have worn a wimple which covered her forehead completely. On her rosary is a gold brooch inscribed with the saying 'Love conquers all'.

---

Ther was also a Nonne, a Prioresse,  
That of hir smiling was ful simple and coy;  
Hire gretteste ooth was but by Seinte Loy;         120  
And she was cleped madame Eglentine.  
Ful weel she soong the service divine,  
Entuned in hir nose ful semely,  
And Frenssh she spak ful faire and fetisly,  
After the scole of Stratford atte Bowe,         125  
For Frenssh of Paris was to hire unknowe,  
At mete wel ytaught was she with alle:  
She leet no morsel from hir lippes falle,  
Ne wette hir fingres in hir sauce depe;  
Wel koude she carie a morsel and wel kepe         130  
That no drope ne fille upon hire brest.  
In curteisie was set ful muchel hir lest.  
Hir over-lippe wiped she so clene  
That in hir coppe ther was no ferthing sene  
Of grece, whan she dronken hadde hir draughte.         135  
Ful semely after hir mete she raughte.  
And sikerly she was of greet desport,  
And ful plesaunt, and amiable of port,

And peyned hire to countrefete cheere
Of court, and to been estatlich of manere, 140
And to ben holden digne of reverence.
But, for to speken of hire conscience,
She was so charitable and so pitous
She wolde wepe, if that she saugh a mous
Kaught in a trappe, if it were deed or bledde. 145
Of smale houndes hadde she that she fedde
With rosted flessh, or milk and wastel-breed.
But soore wepte she if oon of hem were deed,
Or if men smoot it with a yerde smerte;
And al was conscience and tendre herte. 150
Ful semely hir wimpul pinched was,
Hir nose tretis, hir eyen greye as glas,
Hir mouth ful smal, and therto softe and reed;
But sikerly she hadde a fair forheed;
It was almoost a spanne brood, I trowe; 155
For, hardily, she was nat undergrowe.
Ful fetis was hir cloke, as I was war.
Of smal coral aboute hire arm she bar
A peire of bedes, gauded al with grene,
And theron heng a brooch of gold ful sheene, 160
On which ther was first write a crowned A,
And after *Amor vincit omnia.*
      Another Nonne with hire hadde she,
That was hir chapeleyne, and preestes thre.

| | | | |
|---|---|---|---|
| 120 | **Seinte Loy** St Eligius | 137 | **of greet desport** very merry |
| 123 | **Entuned in hir nose ful semely** intoned through her nose most becomingly | 138 | **amiable of port** had a friendly manner |
| 124 | **fetisly** elegantly | 139-40 | **peyned hire to countrefete cheere/ Of court** was at pains to imitate the manners of the court |
| 127 | **at mete wel ytaught was she** at table she demonstrated her careful study of etiquette | 140 | **estatlich** dignified |
| 132 | **In curtesie was set ful muchel hir lest** good manners were very important to her | 141 | **ben holden digne of reverence** be held worthy of respect |
| 134 | **ferthing** speck | 149 | **yerde** stick |
| 136 | **Ful semely after hir mete she raughte** she was most gracious in the way she reached out for her food | | **smerte** sharply, painfully |
| | | 151 | **pinched** pleated |
| | | 152 | **tretis** well formed |

# The Nun's Priest

In the Epilogue to The Nun's Priest's Tale many gaps in our knowledge about him are suddenly filled. He has given a lively telling of his tale (a good actor?), a contrast to the 'hevinesse' of the Monk's story, and is complimented by the Host:

'I-blessed be thy breche and every stoon,
This was a murie tale of Chauntecleer.' (lines 682/3)

The Host gives a physical description of him and speculates on his sexual prowess:

'So gret a nekke, and swich a large breest,
He loketh as a sperhauk with his yen;' (lines 690/1)

'But by my trouthe, if thou were seculer,
Thou woldest ben a trede-foul aright.' (lines 684/5)

You may feel that this is not the man Chaucer has presented throughout this tale. There are various theories about the Epilogue. One suggests that the Priest is simply a body-guard for the nuns, but this does not fit with the way he tells his tale. The Host could simply be poking fun at this priest, on his poor horse, in the company of the Prioress in her fine cloak; and in the convent, confined with all the holy sisters yet unable to perform as Chauntecleer does with all his 'sustres'. A more mundane explanation is that Chaucer did not intend to use the Epilogue. After he had written it, he discarded it and used the sexual jokes – more appropriately – about the Monk instead:

'Thou woldest han been a tredefowel aright.'
(Prologue to The Monk's Tale, line 56)

In addition to the Nun's Priest there are several other pilgrims whose calling is apparently to the religious life: the Prioress and the nun; the Monk; the Friar; the Summoner; the Pardoner and the Parson. In terms of social status, the Nun's Priest is low down the scale, although above the Parson. The Parson is one of the few completely good characters in *The Canterbury Tales*, an ideal priest, devoted to his parishioners. In contrast, it seems that those representatives of the church who are higher up the social scale are on very low rungs of the spiritual ladder. The Friar is skilled at extracting money from people, and the Monk enjoys the good life, but only in a material sense. The Summoner and the Pardoner are corrupt creatures, using their positions to suck money from the poor. The Prioress feeds her pet dogs on best quality bread, but Chaucer never mentions her giving food to any poor people.

The Nun's Priest's character is known to the reader mostly from what he says and how he says it; there is little direct description of him. There is no reason to think ill of him, and clearly he is educated. He seems to have an opinion about the Prioress, shown slyly from time to time. The chase shows that Chaucer has endowed him with a considerable sense of humour.

# Chaucer's pilgrims

*The Canterbury pilgrims leaving the Tabard Inn at Southwark*

*In order of appearance:*

| | |
|---|---|
| **The Knight** | brave, devout and unassuming – the perfect gentleman |
| **The Squire** | in training to follow in the knight, his father's, footsteps, a fine and fashionable young man, and madly in love |
| **The Yeoman** | the knight's only servant, a skilled bowman and forester |
| **The Prioress** | a most ladylike head of a nunnery; she takes great pains with her appearance and manners; she loves animals. She is accompanied by another nun and three priests, the nun and one priest also telling tales |
| **The Monk** | fine and prosperous looking, well-mounted; he loves hunting |
| **The Friar** | cheerful and sociable, he is skilled at obtaining alms from those he visits, particularly the ladies |
| **The Merchant** | rather secretive; his main interest is commerce |
| **The Clerk** | thin and shabby, his passion is scholarship; he spends all he has on books |
| **The Sergeant at Law** | a judge at the assize courts; one of the few pilgrims about whom Chaucer says very little |
| **The Franklin** | a wealthy and hospitable landowner and a JP; but not a member of the aristocracy |
| **The Five Guildsmen** | although they pursue different crafts or trades, they belong to the same social guild – rather self-important townsfolk |
| **The Cook** | he has been brought along to provide meals for the guildsmen; although he is a versatile cook, Chaucer suggests his personal hygiene could be improved |
| **The Shipman** | a weather-beaten master mariner |

| | |
|---|---|
| **The Doctor of Physic** | finely dressed and a skilled medical practitioner; he is an expert in astrology and natural magic; he loves gold |
| **The Wife of Bath** | skilled at weaving; her chief claim to fame is her five husbands |
| **The Parson** | the only truly devout churchman in Chaucer's group; he avoids all the tricks unscrupulous clerics used to get rich, and spends his care and energy on his parishioners |
| **The Ploughman** | the parson's brother and, like him, a simple, honest hard-working man |
| **The Miller** | tough, ugly and a cheat |
| **The Manciple** | responsible for organising the provisions for the lawyers in one of the Inns of Court – clearly a plum job for a clever man |
| **The Reeve** | unsociable, but able; the estate manager of a young nobleman |
| **The Summoner** | an official of a church court; corrupt, lewd and offensive |
| **The Pardoner** | another unpleasant churchman – he earns money by selling 'pardons' from Rome, and by letting simple folk see the fake holy relics he carries |
| **The Host** | the genial landlord of 'The Tabard', who accompanies them on the pilgrimage, and organises the story-telling |
| **Geoffrey Chaucer** | he depicts himself as rather shy and unassuming. |

They are later joined by another story-teller – **The Canon's Yeoman**, a servant whose tale betrays his master's obsessive interest in alchemy.

*A modern pilgrim at Compostela, Spain*

# Pilgrims and pilgrimages

Pilgrimages are journeys made to sacred places, usually as acts of religious devotion. They became increasingly popular during the twelfth and thirteenth centuries, at the time when the threats to the Christian world from infidels and heathens, as Chaucer would have described them, reached their height. The passion to defend and reaffirm the power of the Christian church manifested itself in Crusades to the Holy Land, and an upsurge in religious fervour. Shrines were established in many European countries in places of great religious significance. In England, Canterbury Cathedral was the site of the assassination of Archbishop Becket; Walsingham in Norfolk became a holy site of pilgrimage after visions of the Virgin Mary had been seen there. The great cathedral city of Cologne was another centre of pilgrimage, as was Compostela. Further afield, many pilgrims made the long journey to Jerusalem, available for visits from Christian pilgrims after the Emperor Frederick II had negotiated peace with the 'infidels', and had himself crowned king of the holy city.

Pilgrims (travelling in groups for companionship and safety) would travel to shrines at home and abroad to celebrate their devotion to the church, to seek pardon for their sins, and to ask favours of the saint whose relics were preserved in that place. The traditional image of a pilgrim is of one who travels humbly and simply, dressed in plain clothes, often on foot, carrying a staff. The emblem of a pilgrim is the scallop or cockle shell, worn on cap or hood. This was particularly the symbol of St James, patron saint of military crusaders, and the journey to his shrine in Compostela, northern Spain, was, and still is, one of the great pilgrim routes across Europe. The shells may originally have been real ones, but were later moulded in lead, as were most other pilgrim badges.

By the time Chaucer decided to use a group of pilgrims as a framework for his *Canterbury Tales*, reasons for pilgrimage had become less exclusively devotional. It was certainly a profitable business for enterprising people, as well as a popular pastime. The tourist industry began to take off. The Venetians offered a regular ferry service carrying travellers to and from the Holy Land. The monks of Cluny, the greatest religious house in France, ran a string of hostels along the entire route between their monastery and Compostela. Travel guides were produced, giving information about accommodation available along the route. One for Compostela contained useful Basque vocabulary, and a description of what to see in the cathedral. Horse dealers did a healthy trade hiring out horses to pilgrims.

There was great competition for popular relics between the religious establishments, which sometimes led to rather obvious forgeries. At least two places, for instance, claimed to possess the head of John the Baptist. Pilgrims began to bring home their own souvenirs, and to house them in their local churches, like the fourteenth century traveller William Wey, who proudly deposited in his Wiltshire village church his maps, a reproduction of St Veronica's handkerchief, which he had rubbed on the pillars of 'the tempyl of Jerusalem', and a large number of stones picked up in sites around the Holy Land. His parish priest was presumably delighted. Badges and emblems made of lead were sold at shrines, and eagerly purchased as souvenirs by travellers – the cockle shell for St James, the palm tree from Jericho. At Canterbury it was possible to buy an assortment of badges – an image of the head of the saint, St Thomas riding a horse, a little bell, or a small ampulla [bottle] to hold sacred water. Permission was given from Rome for the local religious houses to obtain a licence to manufacture these.

Some of Chaucer's pilgrims seem to have genuinely devout reasons for visiting Canterbury: the Knight, for instance, has come straight from his military expeditions abroad, fighting for Christendom, and his simple coat is still stained from its contact with his coat of mail. On the other hand, the Wife of Bath, although an enthusiastic pilgrim, hardly seems to be travelling in a spirit of piety or devotion. She lists the places she has visited like a seasoned traveller determined to visit as many tourist attractions as possible. By using a pilgrimage as the frame on which to hang his stories and characterisations, Chaucer was able to point out the way in which attitudes and standards were changing and old values were being lost.

*Geoffrey Chaucer*

# Geoffrey Chaucer

## BIOGRAPHICAL NOTES

**1340?**  The actual date of his birth is uncertain, but he was near 60 when he died. His father and grandfather were both vintners – wealthy London merchants, who supplied wines to the king's court.

Chaucer was introduced to court life in his teens. By the age of 16 he was employed in the service of the wife of the king's son, Lionel, later Duke of Clarence.

**1359**  He fought in France in the army of Edward III. He was captured and imprisoned, but released on payment of his ransom by the duke.

Chaucer was clearly valued by the king and other members of the royal family. In the **1360s** and **1370s** he was sent on diplomatic missions to France, Genoa, Florence and Lombardy.

**1360s**  He married Philippa de Roet, a maid-in-waiting to Edward III's wife, Queen Philippa. His wife's half-sister was Katherine Swynford, third wife of John of Gaunt. The link with this powerful Duke of Lancaster was an important one; the duke was Chaucer's patron and in later life gave Chaucer a pension of £10 a year.

**1368?**  Chaucer wrote *The Book of the Duchess*, a poem on the death of the Duchess Blanche, first wife of John of Gaunt.

**1374**  The position of Comptroller of Customs for the port of London was given to Chaucer, and in the same year the king granted him a pitcher of wine daily. Other lucrative administrative posts became his later.

**1374?**  Chaucer began his unfinished work *The House of Fame*.

**1382?**  Chaucer wrote *The Parlement of Fowles* – possibly for the marriage of Richard II.

**1386**  Like the Franklin in *The Canterbury Tales*, Chaucer was appointed 'Knight of the Shire' or Parliamentary representative for the county of Kent.

**Early 1380s**  He wrote *Troilus and Criseyde*.

It seems that, in spite of the royal and noble patronage he enjoyed, Chaucer was an extravagant man, and money slipped through his fingers. In **1389** he was appointed Clerk of the King's Works by Richard II, but the position lasted only two years.

Richard later gave him a pension of £20 for life, which Chaucer frequently asked for 'in advance'. Threats of arrest for non-payment of debts were warded off by letters of protection from the crown.

**1388?**  Chaucer probably began to formulate his ideas for *The Canterbury Tales* around this time.

**1391**  He was appointed deputy forester (an administrative post) in Petherton, Somerset, and may have spent some time there.

| | |
|---|---|
| **1399** | Henry IV, son of John of Gaunt, became king, and Chaucer was awarded a new pension of 40 marks (about £26), which allowed him to live his few remaining months in comfort. |
| **1400** | Chaucer died in October, and was buried in Westminster Abbey. |

## CHAUCER THE WRITER AND SCHOLAR

Geoffrey Chaucer was actively involved in diplomatic life, moving in court circles, and travelling extensively; he was also an extremely well-read man. His writing shows the influence of classical authors, as well as more recent French and Italian works. The wide range of biblical, classical and contemporary literary references in *The Canterbury Tales*, especially in The Wife of Bath's Prologue and Tale, bear witness to his learning, and he confesses to owning 60 books – a very considerable library in those days. Many of the ideas and themes which occur in *The Canterbury Tales* have been adapted from the works of classical and contemporary sources known to Chaucer and to at least some of his audiences.

His earliest works, such as *The Book of the Duchess*, show the influence of courtly and allegorical French love poetry, in particular the *Roman de la Rose*, a dream poem about the psychology of falling in love. *The Book of the Duchess* is a dream poem in this tradition.

*The House of Fame,* an unfinished narrative poem, shows influences from Chaucer's reading in Italian as well as French poetry. Chaucer is almost the only writer of the century outside Italy to show knowledge of the *Divine Comedy* of Dante (1265–1321), but in this poem, he challenges Dante's claim that it is possible to know the truth about people's actions and motives in the past. Chaucer also admired the writings of two other Italians, Petrarch and Boccaccio; the latter's *Decameron* employs the linking device (in his case a group of sophisticated men and women, entertaining one another with story-telling in a country retreat, whilst the Black Death rages in Florence) that Chaucer was to use later with far greater subtlety, variety and skill.

In both *Troilus and Criseyde,* a re-telling of the tale of love and betrayal at the time of the Trojan War, and in *The Canterbury Tales,* Chaucer shows the debt he owed to classical writers, in particular Ovid and Virgil. He was also familiar with the Bible and some of the writings of theologians highly respected in the Middle Ages, such as St Jerome and St Augustine. He greatly admired the Roman philosopher Boethius, whose work *De Consolatione Philosophiae* (The Consolation of Philosophy) he translated from its original Latin into English. His writing shows an interest in astronomy and astrology, and he wrote one of the very first textbooks in English, *A Treatise on the Astrolabe,* explaining the workings of this astronomical instrument for 'little Lewis', presumably a young son who died in infancy – we hear nothing of him later.

# The Tale told by the Nun's Priest

The story of the fox and the cockerel is not an original one. Beast fables are part of a very long world tradition of spoken and written stories. A modern example is George Orwell's *Animal Farm*. They have been widely illustrated in woodcuts, paintings, carvings and cartoons. In these fables, animals are used to represent human characteristics in order to make a moral point. One of the best known collections of such fables is supposed to have been written by a Greek slave, Aesop, in the sixth century BC. A fox appears in several of them, often in search of food. In one, he tricks a raven into dropping a piece of cheese by flattering him into opening his beak to sing.

Chaucer is likely to have used the French epic *Roman de Renart* as a source for The Nun's Priest's Tale, but has changed various aspects. You might like to consider why he made these alterations.

**Roman de Renart**

a) Chantecler's favourite hen is Pinte. They are owned by a wealthy peasant, Constant de Noues.

b) Reynard gets into the farmyard through a broken fence.

c) The hens see Reynard hiding in the cabbages and run away. Chantecler laughs at them when they tell him of their fear.

d) Chantecler dreams of a creature in a red cloak with a collar of bones. He is forced to put on the cloak, which begins to choke him. He tells Pinte of the dream, which she interprets as meaning the fox will catch Chantecler.

e) Chantecler laughs at Pinte's interpretation of his dream.

**The Nun's Priest's Tale**

a) Chauntecleer's favourite hen is Pertelote. They are owned by a poor widow, Malkin.

b) Daun Russell the fox breaks through the fence.

c) The fox remains well hidden until ready to attack Chauntecleer.

d) Chauntecleer dreams of the red, yellow and black creature and is afraid. Pertelote tells him he needs to take some laxatives to avoid having bad dreams.

e) Chauntecleer eventually decides to ignore the warning of his dream.

The ideas of the fox flattering the cockerel into singing and later the fox being persuaded to speak to the people are found in *Renart* and in another of Aesop's fables. It has been suggested that the traitorous villain of this tale – the fox with black markings – was inspired by Nicholas Colfax, (which could be read as 'Coal-fox') who had been involved in the murder of the Duke of Gloucester in 1397. It is possible that Chaucer is making a political allusion here.

Some people have suggested that the fox in Chaucer's version stands for the devil and the enclosed yard represents the Garden of Eden, but you may feel that to see two chickens as Adam and Eve stretches the concept too far.

Only a small percentage of the Tale is spent on the story of Chauntecleer. Here is an outline of the way the Tale is divided.

*lines*

| | |
|---|---|
| 55-115 | Description of the widow, Chauntecleer and Pertelote. |
| 116-141 | *Chauntecleer's adventure: part 1.* His dream. |
| 142-203 | Pertelote's response. |
| 204-384 | Chauntecleer's long list of examples of warning dreams. |
| 385-438 | *Chauntecleer's adventure: part 2.* He rejects the warning in his dream. The scene is set. Chauntecleer is suddenly afraid. |
| 439-448 | Sermon on the brief nature of earthly happiness. |
| 449-457 | *Chauntecleer's adventure: part 3.* The fox arrives. |
| 458-500 | Digressions on treachery and predestination. |
| 501-558 | *Chauntecleer's adventure: part 4.* The fox flatters Chauntecleer. |
| 559-564 | Sermon on flattery. |
| 565-571 | *Chauntecleer's adventure: part 5.* He is captured. |
| 572-608 | Digressions and lamentations. |
| 609-635 | *Chauntecleer's adventure: part 6.* The chase. |
| 636-638 | Reminder of the fickleness of Fortune. |
| 639-669 | *Chauntecleer's adventure: part 7.* He escapes. |
| 670-680 | Moral messages. |

## Activities

• The language used for different sections of the Tale can vary sharply. Look for instance at the transition from the realism of the farmyard details, 'Pekke hem up right' (line 201) to the earnest reference to 'Daun Catoun' (line 205). It is a beast fable of a very pointed kind.

• Take the whole of Chauntecleer's first story (lines 219-96) and make a sound recording of it. There are three acting role, plus a narrator. Lines 284-91 could be assigned to a minister of justice. Pay close attention to the language used and make your recording as dramatic as possible. Carefully chosen sound effects would help add atmosphere.

• Go through the sections of the Tale listed opposite, deciding how you would briefly describe the language in each, giving examples to support your decisions. Look too, to see how sermons are inserted at various stages in the Tale, sometimes because it was conventional to do so, sometimes to heighten tension or comment on the action.

• A medieval sermon followed fairly rigid guidelines. Looking at the outline of The Nun's Priest's Tale, decide whether you think the whole piece has been designed to be a sermon. The format for sermons is set out below and you may be able to see how Chaucer has adapted it for the Nun's Priest.
  – the main theme, usually biblical. Could this priest's be to 'be murie'?
  – introduction
  – a story (or several) to illustrate the theme
  – developing and explaining the theme
  – how the theme applies to people's lives
  – conclusion and a blessing.

# The power of the church

The church exerted its influence over all aspects of fourteenth century society and life.

- Everyone was expected to attend mass and other services, to make regular confessions and to give offerings to the church.
- Such hospitals and schools as existed were run by monasteries, which also offered hospitality to travellers.
- Almost the only drama in people's lives came from the ritual of the mass; from church music (see lines 85-6); from the depiction of biblical scenes in church wall paintings and stained glass windows and from listening to sermons. (See page 73 for information on sermons.)
- Monastic orders had been gathering vast estates over many centuries – usually left to them by pious landowners. They employed many lay people to help run them and sublet much land. The monks themselves comprised less than half the population of the monasteries in the fourteenth century. In the great cathedral towns such as York and Canterbury, and in the areas controlled by the largest and wealthiest monasteries, the church had considerable control over the population, not just spiritually, but over incomes, housing and food supplies.
- One third of the country's wealth was in the hands of the church.
- Convents were filled with upper class women. Unlike the lower and middle classes it was not considered suitable for rich women to earn a living, so if they failed to find husbands the only alternative was to enter a nunnery, whether or not they had a religious calling.
- The church had real political power. Well into the fourteenth century the position of Chancellor, treasurer of the realm, was a post usually held by a churchman – whose allegiance belonged not only to the king, but to the Pope. St Thomas of Canterbury was a cleric whose dilemma in the post led to his murder in 1170.
- Church courts of law had considerable privileges. The clergy could not be tried and sentenced in the ordinary law courts, whatever their crime, and the church courts gave them protection not available to others, including the right of appeal to the Pope.

## GROWING DISCONTENT

The fourteenth century was a time of considerable upheaval against the long-established tradition of church power. Priests, monks, friars and nuns often provided very poor examples to the laity, falling far short of their religious ideals. The dominance of the centuries-old church institutions was challenged several times in Chaucer's lifetime.

## THE PEASANTS' REVOLT

When the Peasants' Revolt shook the country in 1381, many of the complaints voiced by its leaders were against the oppressive power of the old landlords, including the church.

- The powerful monasteries in the south-east of England were ferociously attacked.
- The rebel leader. Wat Tyler, beheaded the Archbishop of Canterbury on Tower Hill. For more information on the Revolt see pages 54-5.

# Peasants and the life of Chaucer's widow

The term 'peasants' is sometimes used by historians to describe the lowest estate (or class) of medieval people. The word seems to lump together a large number of people as if all their lives were exactly the same. In The Nun's Priest's Tale Chaucer gives a vivid portrait of an individual whose name appears to be Malkyn (short for Mathilda) and who works hard to support herself and her family.

The very poorest people lived in tent-shaped hovels constructed from wooden posts, filled in with wattle, turf or clay. Chaucer's widow is somewhat better off. She lives with her daughters in a two-roomed cruck cottage. The wood for the two large timbers (crucks) joined together at the roof ridge may have been easily obtained since she lives 'Biside a grove'. She is not rich enough to afford glass, so her windows are simply shuttered. Neither does she have a wall chimney, so the interior is 'sooty' because it has a central fire and the smoke has to escape through a hole in the roof. She owns a few animals, and we know Chauntecleer and the hens have a perch in the 'halle'. Had there been three rooms the third would have housed her other livestock. The animals provide her with a few eggs, milk, bacon for grilling, and wool to be wound on her distaff. Bees supplied a valuable addition to the medieval diet. Sugar was expensive and honey was used in making mead, one of the staple drinks of the lower classes. The widow also grows vegetables and perhaps medicinal herbs, but her landholding is not sufficient for her needs and she also works in the dairy of the lord of the manor.

*A reconstruction of a cruck long-house, a much bigger dwelling than the widow's cottage*

# Styles of writing

Chaucer uses a variety of styles of writing, moving successfully from one to another with speed and maintaining his audience's interest.

*Rhetoric: shown as the source of power (sword) and pleasure ('flowers' of poetry); her admirers include Aristotle, Seneca and Justinian*

## RHETORIC

Rhetoric was an art and technique derived from classical Greek and Roman models. It was one of the seven liberal arts taught at medieval universities, the others being Grammar, Logic, Music, Arithmetic, Geometry and Astronomy. A medieval rhetorician dealt with the structure and style of writing and speaking effectively and entertainingly. A famous example is Geoffrey de Vinsauf (Gaufred) who wrote *Poetria Nova* (New Poetry). Chaucer uses the rhetorical techniques he writes of throughout The Nun's Priest's Tale, and refers to him in line 441, 'a rethor'. De Vinsauf's description of the accidental killing of Richard I by one of his own men in 1199 was famous and was probably so well known because many people had heard the extract, although they might not have read the whole book. These few lines give a flavour of the account. They are an example of apostrophe, i.e. a speech addressed to someone or something that is not actually there.

> In time of grief, express your grief with these words:
> Once defended by King Richard's shield, now undefended, O England, bear witness to your woes in the gestures of sorrow. Let your eyes flood with tears, and pale grief waste your features. Let writhing anguish twist your fingers, and woe make your heart within bleed. Let your cry strike the heavens. Your whole being dies in his death; the death was not his but yours. Death's rise was not in one place only, but general. O tearful day of Venus! O bitter star! That day was your night; and that Venus your venom.

Look back to page 51 to see how Chaucer makes use of this account. You could think

76

about why Chaucer uses various rhetorical devices for this tale of the farmyard. Consider the following:

- Does the Nun's Priest want to impress his listeners? (Possibly the Prioress particularly, as he is perhaps better educated than she is.)
- Is Chaucer making fun of rhetoricians?
- Does the use of rhetoric make the modern audience take the moral of the Tale more – or less – seriously?
- Do the digressions used help maintain tension and enlarge the Tale, or do they dissipate tension? Perhaps Chaucer has both effects in mind?

Here are brief descriptions of some rhetorical techniques:

### Amplification
This is used to make your subject seem more important. The devices of Description and Comparison are used in the first description of Chauntecleer (lines 83-98).

### Digressions
The story of Chauntecleer's adventure takes up only a small part of the Tale; most of the Priest's time is spent on digressions of various types. Digressions were an important aspect of a rhetorician's art, giving the opportunity to illustrate a point with examples – and to demonstrate learning. All digressions were supposed to help support and develop arguments, and were not intended simply to allow for showing off. Consider whether all the Priest's digressions move along his main points.

**Circumlocutio** This technique is a roundabout way of saying something in order to impress, for example the longwinded calculation of the date of Chauntecleer's adventure (lines 421-31).

**Exclamatio/apostrophe** These devices, employed to show the audience the emotional state of a character, and used in the Tale in the lament for Chauntecleer, were common in sermons and so are appropriate for the Nun's Priest, since he would be used to preparing sermons for the nuns. (See example above from *Poetria Nova*.)

**Exemplum** Chauntecleer uses many examples of dreams to try to persuade Pertelote to his point of view.

**Occupatio** This technique involves informing your audience that you will not tell them something, while in fact outlining the main points of what you want them to know. Find an example.

## MOCK HEROIC
A classic heroic (or epic) poem features a brave and noble hero who undertakes great deeds for his country. The gods may assist him, or let him suffer. Homer's *Illiad* and *Odyssey* are two major works in this tradition.

The mock heroic uses the same format as the heroic poem but its intention is not to glorify a real hero, but to mock an event or a person, by using an overblown style. Find examples of effective use of the mock heroic in the Tale.

# Question and themes

Use these questions and suggestions as a basis for written work or group discussion.

1 WHO TELLS THE TALE?
 The Nun's Priest's Tale has been described as the most 'Chaucerian' of all the stories in *The Canterbury Tales*, partly because there are so many little tales within it. At various stages different voices are used by Chaucer.
  a) Identify sections of the Tale which you feel belong to each of these 'voices':
    • Chaucer the writer
    • Chaucer the character in *The Canterbury Tales* for example, in the Nun's Priest's Prologue
    • The Nun's Priest
    • Chauntecleer.
      What is achieved by the changes of narrator?
  b) Choose a section containing more than one 'voice' and prepare a reading to give to your group.

2 LITERARY TECHNIQUES
  a) Many people choose this tale as their favourite out of the whole *Canterbury Tales*. One of the reasons is the variety of humorous approaches in it. Identify and evaluate examples of: satire; mocking of pride; double meanings; self delusion; mock heroic; parody.
  b) There are several mini-sermons in the Tale. Decide which are designed particularly to give useful moral teaching, and which are simply a conventional literary flourish.
  c) Show how the use of techniques of rhetoric adds to the interest of the Tale.
  d) How far and in what ways does the use of realistic, down-to-earth detail enhance your enjoyment of the Tale?
  e) Do you appreciate the Tale more for its satire or for its sermons?
  f) Choose your favourite examples of Chaucer's vivid descriptive language.
  g) There are many examples of dialogue and direct speech in the Tale. Show how they help to indicate character.

3 MALE/FEMALE RELATIONSHIPS
  a) How are the characters of Chauntecleer and Pertelote developed throughout the Tale? What points are made about the differing attitudes and behaviour of male and female to the various topics and events of the Tale? How far do these differences persist today?
  b) What is the effect of the disclaimer in lines 494-500? Who is speaking at this point?

4 **MEDIEVAL LIFE**

a) What do we learn from the Tale about medieval life? Consider: the social order; beliefs; everyday life. Which aspects are strange, and which are familiar to a modern audience?

b) What indications are there of Chaucer's learning throughout the Tale?

c) The Nun's Priest is supposed to be telling his story to a group of pilgrims from a wide variety of social backgrounds – from the Knight to the Ploughman. Find indications in the Tale which show what sort of courtly audience Chaucer was really writing for.

5 **THE MORAL OF THE TALE**

a) There are many 'morals' in the Tale, one of which is that we should avoid complacency. Choose two lines which you feel illustrate this.

b) 'For he that wynketh whan he sholde see
Al wilfully, God lat him nevere thee!' (lines 665/6)
Both Chauntecleer and the fox, whether literally or metaphorically, suffer as a result of closing their eyes. Find examples of characters in Chauntecleer's stories about dreams who are blind to messages – often with fatal consequences.

c) Throughout the Tale pride is shown to lead to dire consequences. Make a list of characters whose pride leads them into suffering. In addition, look to see where pride and vanity are subtly criticised in those who think of themselves as learned.

d) 'Taketh the fruit, and lat the chaf be stille.' (line 677) Is this simply 'a murie tale' or is there more to it? Some critics have suggested that the 'chaf' is more worthwhile than the 'fruit'. (The Host reminds us in the Prologue to the Tale that some 'chaf' is necessary to keep the attention of your audience.) There are certainly many examples of wit and humour throughout the Tale.

6 **CHAUCER'S LANGUAGE**

Now that you have got to grips with Chaucerian English, how much have you enjoyed it? Any difficulties you have had would have been understood by Chaucer. In his long poem *Troilus and Criseyde* he wrote:

Ye know ek that in forme of speche is chaunge
Withinne a thousand yeer, and wordes tho        (**tho** then)
That hadden pris, now wonder nyce and straunge  (**pris** value)
Us thinketh hem, and yet thei spake hem so,
And spedde as wel in love as men now do;
(Book II lines 22-26)

# Glossary of frequently-used words

| | | | |
|---|---|---|---|
| aferd | afraid | nas (ne was) | was not |
| anon | immediately | natheless | none the less |
| bad | advised | noot (ne woot) | know not |
| bifel | it happened | reccheless | careless, imprudent |
| certes | certainly | seith | says |
| cleped | called | shrewen | curse |
| conseil | advice | sikerly | certainly |
| drede | fear | sin | since |
| eek | also | sooth | truth, truly |
| everichon | everyone | swevene | dream |
| ful | very | swich | such |
| han | have | wight | person |
| hente | catch, seize | winke | close the eyes |
| highte | named | witing | knowledge |
| hire | their | wroght | done |
| lo | look | yet | still |
| met, mette | dreamed | ynough | enough |
| muche, muchel | many, much | ywis | certainly |
| namo, namoore | no more | | |
| narwe | small (*literally,* narrow) | | |